Must I Really Go, Lord?

Betty N. Bisset

Published by GOSPEL FOLIO PRESS
304 Killaly Street West
Port Colborne, ON, L3K 6A6
Canada

ISBN 1-897117-03-5

Sketches drawn by Malcolm Bisset
Map drawn by Gordon Bisset

Cover design by Daveen Lidstone

ORDERING INFORMATION:
Gospel Folio Press
Phone: 1-800-952-2382
E-mail: orders@gospelfolio.com

Printed in the United States of America

CONTENTS

Acknowledgments

Many friends have had a part in the preparation of this book. I wish I could list all those who have helped simply by encouraging me to write. My mother was the first by keeping many of my letters, then the late Mr. G.C.D. Howley, one of the elders of my Assembly, who commended me to missionary service and who first said, "Betty, this is a book!" Much more recently there are those who, like my long suffering husband, kindly read, commented on and corrected the manuscript. They are: Mrs. Ethel Renwick, Mr. Paul Young of 'Echoes of Service,' Alison Browning and Gertrud Harlow. Some practical hints and encouragement came from Dr. John Andrews and from our son-in-law, Peter Camilleri.

The book would not be possible but for those who are included in the story, and I trust that if it falls into their hands, they will be happy with what they read.

I would like to dedicate the book to my parents, Mr. and Mrs. Harold Miles and, of course, to Gordon, in the Lord's goodness, my husband for 47 years, so far.

Preface

This book is a pleasure to read—and also a challenge. The writer's sense of humour will bring many a smile to your face—perhaps even make you chuckle as it did me.

The Lord's hand is evident througout, leading, protecting, supplying, filling with joy, strengthening and upholding in difficulty. It brings glory to our wonderful God! As you read, your own faith will be strengthened by Betty's frequent testimony to the Lord's goodness and faithfulness. And you might even find yourself asking: If He used the Bissets, could He not enable and use me also to take the message of His salvation to needy, hungry hearts?

The book illustrates that the Lord does not call all His servants in the same way—just as no two of us came to the foot of the Cross by the same route, except for one thing: we all heard the Lord saying tenderly, "I have loved you with an everlasting love; Therefore with lovingkindness I have drawn you." (Jer. 31:3) And so we came—how thankful we are that we did and received eternal life.

But the Lord doesn't stop with saving our *souls*. He has purchased us with His blood on the cross. Now we are His and no longer belong to ourselves. He wants our *entire being* for Himself. He wants to be Lord of our lives. And so again He draws and calls. Some of His children respond quickly, others "reluctantly," as did the writer of this book. But she DID answer His call and has never regretted it. How will you respond?

—*Gertrud Harlow*

BRAZIL
L.TITICACA
BOLIVIA
LA PAZ
COCHABAMBA
MONTERO
ORURO
SANTA CRUZ
THE ANDES
SUCRE
POTOSI
UYUNI
TUPIZA
TARIJA
PARAGUAY
VILLAZON
CHILE
ARGENTINA

Introduction

The grey rocks of Land's End slid smoothly toward the horizon, shrank into the misty sea and disappeared. A man's voice beside me broke into my reverie, "Don't worry, they will still be here when you come back!" I managed a watery smile, even to converse with the stranger for a moment or two. How much had he read of my thoughts as I gazed over the rail of the ship back towards the shores of England? I had never ventured abroad before; the Isle of Wight had been my only 'overseas' experience! It was no wanderlust that was taking me away now. I was on my way to be a missionary, and, although the future was uncertain, I had a pathway set before me and a trustworthy Guide. I anticipated all kinds of excitement, adventure and joy, perhaps hardship or even suffering, but as the day wore on I had to combat plain ordinary homesickness. The ship ploughed relentlessly on, widening the distance between myself and every loved person and familiar thing.

I had friends who so wanted to be missionaries. They would gladly have left home and gone overseas at the least intimation from their Lord. So why didn't He call them? Did He really have to call me? I was so happy at home, so completely content with my parents and so full of plans whereby I could serve the Lord. Into the midst of my security came the disrupting, insistent voice of the Lord calling me to the mission field and I was aghast! Excuses crowded into my mind. Above all, how could I leave my parents when I was an only child? It would hurt them too much. Years went by and the "still small voice" could not be ignored. How patient the Lord was with me. I could not understand then His love, His plans, or even the privilege of the service to which He was calling me.

So began the preparations for the mission field; time would not stand still and eventually the great day dawned and I made my way to Euston station to the boat train. It seemed strange that London was going about its business as though nothing exceptional was happening when this was the greatest moment of my life! The train gathered speed, friends' faces blurred and disappeared, my mother and father stepped bravely into a future without their dearly loved daughter and only child, and I began my journey to the unknown land to which the Lord had called me, over a month's journey away.

Foreign travel proved fascinating, and as the grey Atlantic gave place to the blue Caribbean waters, I began to look forward eagerly to the various ports of call: Cuba, Jamaica, Curaçao, Venezuela, Columbia, Panama. The Pacific Ocean, an inky blue sea with a tremendous swell, was quite different in character from the grey Atlantic. We hugged the coast of South America, stopped off at Guayaquil, Ecuador, spent a day in Callao, Lima, Peru, then Arica, and finally Antofagasta, Chile, for the journey up into the mountains of Bolivia. That night I lay in a bed at the Salvation Army Hostel in Antofagasta. I heard the ship's hooter and as she sailed away, homesickness engulfed me once more.

The journey up into Bolivia is a story of adventure—one long tale of kindness, miracles and answers to prayer. So many things began to happen to me that I began to write long letters to my friends in England describing my adventures and recording the Lord's goodness to me. Those letters form the basis of this book. Many of the things mentioned are now commonplace to me and I would write about them differently, but these are the first impressions of a land, a people and a work as seen through the eyes of a very raw missionary. I thought that I had sacrificed all I had for the

Lord, but you will see how, as the years passed, I proved the truth of Mark 10:29, 30 (see below). I have received from the Lord's hand so much more than I ever gave. Time and time again I proved His love as He showered blessings on me. The letter form demands considerable use of the first person and I ask your forgiveness and patience. The book is written solely for the Lord's glory.

His power can make you what you ought to be,
His blood can cleanse your heart and make you free;
His love can fill your soul and you will see
'Twas best for Him to have His way with thee.

(CSSM Chorus 321 Robert Harkness.
Copyright with 'Charles M. Alexander Copyright Trust')

Mark 10:29, 30, Jesus said,

"No one who has left home or brothers or sisters or mother or father or children or fields for me and the gospel will fail to receive a hundred times as much in this present age (homes, brothers, sisters, mothers, children, and fields—and with them, persecutions) and in the age to come, eternal life."

Curriculum Vitae Betty

"I fled Him down the nights and down the days,
I fled Him down the labyrinthine years
Of my own mind"

"Hound of Heaven," by Francis Thompson, is a poem which gripped me because it was my own experience. I didn't want to be a missionary and I did my best to escape the Lord's call! It was alright at first; as a ten-year-old I really wanted to serve the Lord. To be a missionary seemed rather a good idea, and when, at 13, in a Baptist Sunday School, the Y.P. did a play, I had a real pash on the 'missionary' under the palm tree, wearing a topee of course, and teaching the local people. Later though, out riding my bike, I suddenly thought, "That's all right on a platform, but you'd have to leave your parents and friends and go all alone to...where?" I determined definitely NOT to be a missionary and, from then on, I carefully avoided any situation in which the Lord might call me.

On then to age 19; I was an ardent Girl Crusader, junior officer at camps and assistant class leader. The war ended and annual G.C.U. meetings recommenced in London. I was all agog. It wasn't until the tea break (a picnic in the park) that I remembered that the evening session was a missionary one, but there was no escape. I went and, in a saintly sort of way, prayed that the Lord would call some of those girls to be missionaries. He answered my prayer but it also went right home to me. It wasn't in the message that I heard His voice, but we sang (twice!)...

> *"MINE are the hands to do the work,*
> *MY feet shall run for Thee,*
> *MY lips shall sound the glorious news,*
> *Lord, here am I, send ME."*

Could I refuse any longer? I just had to sing that.

Ten more years went by, and sometimes the Lord had to push me step by step. I became a chiropodist (podiatrist) and then a nurse. I didn't want to do nursing and purposely applied to only one hospital where I knew there was a five year waiting list. Mysteriously, a vacancy occurred and the matron fitted me in straight away! More than once I thought I was in love but I stuck to the missionary call and resigned myself to joining the noble band of single ladies on the mission field. I hoped that, once I showed myself willing, the Lord would change His plan for me but, to my surprise, He let me go.

How did I know that I should go to Bolivia? I had been invited to Pweto, Congo. I was interested in Ethiopia and corresponded with missionaries there, but my heart was in South America. A very large map of that continent half filled my bedroom wall and I devoured books about the jungle—but should I go where **I** wanted? How could I know the Lord's will? One day my mother told me on the phone that the elders of the assembly would be writing to me. My heart missed a beat! I wondered if they would say that my health wasn't good enough, or for some other reason I should not go. I waited impatiently, praying that the letter would be the Lord's will for me; to go or stay, and if to go, then where? I trembled when the letter came. The first page I pulled out of the envelope was a leaf torn from a Wycliffe magazine with an article entitled, **"You are invited, can you come? Come to Bolivia."**

In the margin someone had written, "This may be of interest to Betty." The elders asked, "How soon can you go?"

~~~~~~~~~~~~~~~~~~~

So in September 1957, I sailed out past Land's End. I thought I was sacrificing everything for the Lord, but I discovered that He was soon to give me a hundred times more than I had given up and so much more than I ever asked or thought. Not only did He give me the privilege of serving Him in Bolivia, but He led me straight into…but that comes into the story!

—Betty N. Bisset.
~~~~~~~~~~~~~~~~~~~

1
The First Letters

There is a lot to be said for travelling by sea. It may take a long time and some might consider it tedious, but the culture shock is less of a jolt than when flying into a new country, and the mind and body can adapt gradually to the new circumstances. Our many long voyages over the years have enriched our lives with a multitude of experiences, and have given innumerable opportunities to lead Bible studies among other passengers and to witness personally to people from all walks of life.

Here are a few cameos culled from letters written home on the first voyage…

S.S. Reina del Mar, Pacific Steam Navigation Company.
SEPTEMBER 1957

Dear Friends at Home,

I didn't see much of the departure from Liverpool. I was busy eating and putting my cabin to rights. It was very dull and cold on deck, and I was suffering too much from nostalgia to add to it by watching the coast of England slip by in the mist.

This is a lovely boat; it is new and very nicely furnished, even in the Tourist class accommodation. My cabin is about the size of our bathroom at home and has two berths—I am "on the shelf." I had it to myself at first, but on Friday a Spanish lady appeared with a cute little baby. This meant adding a cot for the baby, which left me very little room to move and, as the baby is teething, I've had some very disturbed nights. I love the baby—a real little Spaniard with curly black greased hair, thick gold earings and red pantaloons. Her name is Mercedes or "Cookie, for friend," her mother told me.

Today I was moved to another cabin with an English lady who lives in the Isle of Pines, off Cuba. Hers is a pathetic story of divorce and other tragedie. She is much older than I, but at present she is my "friend." No one would know this was a British boat apart from the fact that we get the B.B.C. Overseas News every day at 6 p.m. The waiters and stewards speak Spanish and only a few of the passengers speak English (in this class anyway!). I'm surrounded by Spanish chatter, which is no doubt very good for me. They seem so excitable and all talk together with raised voices. There are a lot of priests, monks and nuns on board and they walk around chanting. I have some difficulty in getting myself understood and the waiter can't understand why I want water instead of wine—"Dat is for de fish!" he says.

There are also a lot of Jamaicans on board including a group of Scouts returning from a Jamboree. They seem very well-behaved boys and they, of course, speak English. They left one Scoutmaster behind at La Pallice (France) as he went ashore and then missed the boat. Apparently he is a press reporter so I guess he will have a good story! The music these boys play is amazing; they were on deck with drums and maracas and when they dance their limbs are so loose they seem like rubber. They dance leaning backwards and pass under a stick which is gradually lowered, like an inversion of the "high jump." They can sing too. They have a short assembly each morning on deck and I listened nearby. One day they sang, "The King of love my Shepherd is" and it nearly finished me! On another day it was…

"Praise, my soul, the King of Heaven,
To His feet thy tribute bring,
Ransomed, healed, restored, forgiven,

***Who, like me**, His praise should sing?"*

"Who, indeed?" I asked myself, and took courage.

Friday midday found us at Santander on the North coast of Spain—a lovely place. The waiters and stewards were all excited as some would be seeing their wives and families for just four hours. What a life! Four hours together in three months! We arrived in brilliant sunshine, sailing into the middle of this almost circular bay of blue water surrounded by green hills and misty blue mountains, the towns nestling along the waterline. The houses remind me of slab cake, sliced and ready to eat. Small boats and yachts were out from the beaches and holidaymakers in colourful bathing suits waved to us. I loved the way the Spaniards sang as we approached, and the way the lights twinkled on and were reflected in ribbons across the sea as evening fell. The ship was floodlit too, and the white rigging looked like a string of pearls against the blue velvet sky. The water was absolutely still, and Spanish singing reached me across the silence.

We headed out into the Atlantic Ocean towards Bermuda after a short call at La Coruña on the North West coast. Very soon our troubles began. We ran straight into bad weather and had to alter our course to avoid a hurricane. *(We heard later of the sinking of the cadet sailing ship, the 'Pamir.')* We still caught the tail of it, and the wind and seas were tremendous. I wasn't really afraid but I certainly wasn't very happy. Most people were seasick; not surprising as it really is a ghastly sensation. I stood up in the bow of the ship and watched the horizon disappear beneath me and then leap into the air again; it reminded me of a rocking horse in a children's playground. The sea got rougher every minute and I decided it was time to go in. I looked round and realised I was the only person on deck! I had quite a job to get back inside and had to go right 'round the railing hanging on. It would have been impossible to walk across the deck. I learned from a crew member the next day that "the Bridge" had been watching me, really concerned, and they were on the point of sending a sailor to bring me in. It was silly but I was enjoying it until I realised that I was alone. I tried a shower before bed but that was really funny as the ship heaved all over the place. The floor was so slippery I couldn't stand. There was no way I could wash my feet! By morning it was really rough; tremendous waves tossed the ship over great mountains and into deep troughs, and the boat seemed so small in this vast expanse of water. The wind howled through the rigging; I really felt the magnificence of it and marvelled at the power of the Creator, reflecting again on the One who calmed the storm with a word.

If only something would keep still for five minutes! The deck heaves, the lounge chairs bounce, and even to be horizontal on your bunk is like lying on a seesaw. To walk along a corridor is an experience! You walk a little, then plod uphill, suddenly high-stepping as the floor teasingly falls away from you and you find yourself running downhill. You dare not take the stairs two at a time as the step may move away as you aim at it. I just had to stand and laugh at myself but it has made me terribly tired. It was good to see the shadowy outline of the Azores as we passed between them. Two full days of this and now, Wednesday, the sun has come out, blue sky with some clouds, a high wind, a fairly calm deep blue sea with frothy white foam, and we are heading fast for the Tropics, back on course, and it is really beautiful.

Thursday was a perfect day; brilliant blue sea, sunshine, smooth sailing. It begins to feel like a holiday! I must make the most of the warmth as I shall soon be cold. Porpoises are playing around the ship and we've just sighted sharks. The family I first made friends with are most intrigued by my doings, and it was good to be able to tell them about what the Lord means in my life. They were quite amazed to find someone who gave God the first consideration. Evidently I am the topic of conversation over drinks in the bar when, of course, I am not present. I do wonder what they say! The lady with whom I share a cabin has a sad tale of divorce and unfaithfulness right through the family. I was able to tell her about the way of life in Christ and what a personal thing it is that "the Son of God loved me [and He loved **her**] and gave Himself for me" (for us both, individually). I have another week with her as she leaves the ship in Havana. She tells everyone very readily that I am a missionary, so at least that is well known. I sometimes get asked, "What order?" assuming I am some kind of nun! It isn't easy on board as it is such a frivolous life, and to get a quiet time for prayer is very difficult; the evening entertainment often gives me time to be alone. I don't know how people survive in this kind of atmosphere and I long for the freshness and wholesomeness of Christian company.

The long Atlantic crossing is nearly over now and Bermuda is coming up. Land at last…

BERMUDA—Kind Wycliffe missionaries cared for me for the day and made it a memorable occasion. The sea is such a lovely colour, a sort of transparent turquoise, that I could hardly believe it! The taxis were fascinating with their colourful canopies, but the island itself seemed very bare and there were no trees, due to, I believe, a disease of some kind which stripped the island of trees a year or two ago.

Sunday on board is rather nice. All the crew attend the service in the First Class lounge, resplendent in their 'whites.' It was nice to sing some hymns but the sermon was pathetic! I had a long philosophical kind of conversation with a student but he admitted that my simple gospel defeated his arguments.

THE BAHAMAS—What a hot sticky day! It feels like a hothouse at Kew Gardens. We were not able to go ashore but the Island looked beautiful. Little boys rowed out to us and dived into the deep royal blue sea for coins. I have never seen such a blue sea, or sky for that matter.

CUBA—Havana is impressive but going ashore was scary as there seemed to be heavily armed police and soldiers everywhere.

The children are gorgeous and all so beautifully dressed. I went ashore with some friends but didn't like the way the men whistled at me!

JAMAICA—I got to know an American lady with two little girls on the ship so I went ashore with them. We took a bus to Hope gardens, a really lovely park, and enjoyed the unfamiliar trees and magnificent flowers. I bought a big straw hat with flowers embroidered with raffia on the brim. I like Jamaica. It is all so colourful and bright. There are several missionary families on the boat now and it is lovely to have Christian fellowship. I'm getting used to being 'Auntie.' The children don't understand my English very well and one little boy, on hearing that I had come from England, asked, in an astonished American drawl, "Wow! How did you get **there**?!"

VENEZUELA—We called in at La Guayra on Sunday morning. The whole missionary crowd of us went ashore, but we soon scuttled back to the ship as it was oppressively hot and very noisy as music blared out from all the shops. The evening was better as we set sail again and some of our group organised a hymn-singing session on deck. A musical saw played by one of our number was a great attraction, and several passengers and crew sat around listening. I haven't heard one before. An ordinary carpenter's saw was rested on a stool and played with a violin bow on the straight edge. The saw was bent into a curve to make the different notes. It was a beautiful clear sound.

Next stop—CURACAO—an island in the Dutch West Indies. There was just time for a swim. No problems about 'getting under' here and the sharks were kept at bay by a special fence. So on to the…

PANAMA CANAL—It took us nine hours to pass through the canal and we were on deck all day, just rushing down for meals and back on deck again. There was so much to see! The heat was unbearable (yet this is winter time!) and I spent the whole day in my Jamaican hat. The locks were really interesting. We seemed to have barely inches to spare on either side. Out on the lakes everything is a lush green; the water, the banks, the thick forest; occasionally we saw a monkey. A ship passed in the opposite direction and it seemed as though we could almost reach over and touch the people. It was going to Liverpool, causing me another twinge of homesickness, but I had so much to see and do. The ship was really feeling like home. So...on to the Pacific and the coast of South America.

There was nearly a tragedy in one missionary family. A three year old got hold of a bottle of sea-sickness tablets and took some, giving some to her baby brother as well. Both were semi-conscious for several hours and the baby went into fits but mercifully they are now none the worse.

Now LIMA (Peru)—and oh! I've had such a wonderful time! News of my coming had arrived before me and some American missionaries came to the boat to whisk me off to the Wycliffe Group House. Some of the others came too. What a lovely house it is, and the lawns and flowers made it just perfect. Perry Smith and Billie (his wife) packed a picnic lunch (that's the first time I have ever scrubbed fruit with a nailbrush and soapy water!) and we went off to the beach. It was my idea to swim and they were a bit appalled as it is evidently not the swimming season, but I couldn't resist it and Perry bravely came in with me. The breakers were enormous but it was fun, and the water was no colder than it is on the South coast of England in the summer. We went back to the Group House for dinner and then took the others back to the ship and showed it to Perry and Billie. It looked magnificent with all the lights on and I felt quite proud of it as if I belonged there. I went back with Billie and Perry for the night and next day they showed me round an Indian market. I loved the Indian women with their hair in plaits and babies on their backs. Later, I visited the Wycliffe Museum on the 14th floor of a building in town and saw lovely

Indian things. I was very taken with a feather headdress made of red and yellow feathers woven into a basketwork crown. The arrows and things looked sinister indeed, and I pondered on how wonderful it is that so many of these fierce tribes have come to know Christ as Saviour. Only the power of God could have done this.

After lunch I came back to the boat, said "goodbye" to my new friends, and here I am ready to sail on. I wonder what awaits me now. How wonderful these folk have been to me. I'm nearing the end of my sea trip and I am a bit afraid. I must leave this ship which has been my home for four weeks and set foot ashore alone. I've learned a lot about myself in these weeks, about the sort of person I really am, and I'm not very happy about some things. The Lord has been so wonderful to me—so patient and understanding—He has kept me from falling into temptation. How horribly human I find myself to be. Thank you for your prayers and for your loving support. I've had shoals of letters, causing some teasing comments from the crew! The next step? A train journey alone, from Antofagasta on the coast of Chile up into the mountains of Bolivia, the Andes. Well…

"I can be calm and free from care, on any shore for God is there." (*Madam Guyon*)

2

MOON JOURNEY?

I am still in Antofagasta. The boat docked at about 6 a.m. and while I was eating my breakfast, a grubby looking man appeared demanding, "Señorita Betty." He was the baggage man—I had to show him which was mine (8 pieces!) and which of the boxes could go straight to the railway station. Back to my breakfast. Next a young Englishman appeared (surprise and great relief!) asking for "Miss Miles" (as I then was). He was from the railway company. (*God, who has His people in high places, had made me known to a Christian gentleman, Mr. Ernest Warder, high up in the railway company which was, in those days, British. On arrival at Antofagasta I had received a letter from Mr. Warder, so far unknown to me, and discovered that he had done so much to smooth my path.)* My visitor told me that my ticket had been booked to Potosí (see map on page *viii*) and he bore off my passport to do all the necessary things with that, presumably with the Chilean authorities. I was to have stayed in a hotel, already booked for me, but I was finally taken under the wing of some Swedish Salvation Army workers who were really looking for another missionary couple, who had actually disembarked at the previous port of call, Arica. This was a real provision from the Lord, so here I am, installed in the Salvation Army hostel. My hosts speak no English, so communication is rather difficult with only my few words of Spanish and certainly no Swedish.

The house is rather bare but clean, and I have a comfortable bed; a lovely smell is coming up from the kitchen. I am glad to be here instead of at the 'Hotel Splendid' where I was booked because I had been advised on the boat to avoid it at all costs! The name, they told me, is deceiving.

I had come ashore in a rocky little boat, accompanied by a missionary family, the Strongs. Mr. Strong was indeed a tower of strength. I was so grateful for his help through customs; they treated me very gently. We all piled into a taxi. It was great! It was a brilliant blue, ramshackle car (1930 model) with a canvas roof; it had to be cranked up and the springs popped up all over the place making sitting down quite an experience! My overnight luggage was jammed on the wings behind the headlights and we proceeded erratically to my home for the night, and then on to the station where Mr. Strong and the kind Englishman from the railway company rescued me (in Spanish) from the baggage man who was evidently a bit of a rogue!

I am missing the 'Reina del Mar.' It is so familiar to me now that I can't bear to think of it sailing at 9 p.m. without me. It seemed such an alien place at first but I have become pretty much at home there and have met so many really kind people. There were fifteen letters awaiting me when I arrived in Antofagasta and they were such a joy. They helped me to get over the homesickness. The ship's crew were really jealous! I had the letters in my hand when I went to Immigration, and two of the officers said, "Now we've tracked down the girl who gets all the letters," and when I went to the Purser's office later, the interpreter said, "Don't tell me you've read all those letters already!" It did take me a long time but I relished every word.

The boat is just hooting to say she is ready to sail.

Now I really am a stranger in a strange land.

UYUNI (Bolivia)
20.10.57

No, I certainly didn't expect to be here! *(...another Mr. Warder arrangement as I later discovered)*

The train from Antofagasta was rather fun, a wooden one with an ancient engine, and I and my luggage were duly installed in a sleeping compartment for two. My companion was a Bolivian lady with her baby. With much ringing of bells we pulled out of the station and I had my last glimpse of the sea, probably for some years. I had been introduced to a British gentleman and his Argentine wife *(more railway people)* and they were wonderful to me on the journey. They took me along to the dining car and insisted on treating me as their guest for all meals. This was wonderful for me as I had little Chilean money left and was wondering how I would pay for meals. They helped in another way too; the Bolivian lady in my compartment was desperately sick (from the increasing altitude) and when my new Argentine friend came to look for me she said, "My dear, you can't sleep in here. Come along with me." She took me to her compartment and her husband very kindly moved out to sleep elsewhere.

The handbook of South America describes this journey as resembling a trip across the moon, and that is just the way it is. It is just indescribably barren. Through the train window I can see desert...sand...stones...extinct volcanoes...lava...smoking volcanoes...mountains. There is not a blade of grass, tree or animal to be seen—just barrenness everywhere. There are odd little graves where people died building the railway and whole cemeteries with not a house in sight. It is eerie, weird—almost frightening. The railway is perilous in places as the line takes sharp turns on high banks with what seems like only a few inches to spare on either side. Surprisingly there are one or two straggling villages on this wilderness journey. It was very hot all day and dazzling to look out of the window because of the terrific glare from the sun and the sand.

After 6 p.m. the sun began to go down and the colours were just magnificent; the mountain tops were all glowing orange then purple, blue and pink. It was also intensely cold, so on went the woollies and coat. I haven't had a headache or sickness but I do feel very tired. I am at 12,000 feet now and am taking things very quietly.

At the border station, when I was tucked up and asleep, I was awakened to hear my name! A missionary gentleman was looking for me along the train. I didn't know who he was (Mr. Willie Hill from Scotland and working in Uyuni) but he had come this far to meet me and he had me all organised! The plan was to introduce me gradually to the high altitude by staying for a few days in Uyuni before going on to Potosí. At 2 a.m. we got off the train and it was, as someone said, 'cold enough to freeze the ears off a brass monkey!" I was taken to the house of yet more British 'railway' people. They were away and had kindly allowed me to use their home. It was luxurious, with central heating, lovely furniture, comfy beds and, oh joy, a super bathroom! Here I was left and I couldn't believe it. I was filthy dirty from the train so I wallowed in a hot bath and got into bed at 3 a.m.

This morning I had a lovely English breakfast with a Mr. Thompson who lived next door, and at 10 a.m. Mr. Hill came for me and took me to his house, a real contrast. Back to missionary realities. At present they have only a room with a Christian family, and the house really is pathetic. Part of it has only a dirt floor and the furniture is poor; they just have so little, but they are so happy in the Lord and are hoping for a house soon. Believe it or not, the only toilet for them and for the Indian family is the chicken run! The family had scrubbed up especially for the benefit of the new Señorita but they still looked pretty grubby to me. I soon made friends with the four children. The man is a real support of the little Christian assembly and took much part in the meetings.

At the meeting in the afternoon my letter of commendation was read out, translated into Spanish by Mr. Hill, and it seemed so strange to come from my large and flourishing home church to this little group of Bolivian Indians. There were about 14 of us and it was a lovely time even though it was well beyond my understanding of Spanish. There was a gospel meeting in the evening; ever so many people came in late but, in spite of that, they greeted everyone, "Buenas noches" and shook hands with the preacher before they sat down! The light went out in the middle of the meeting and Mrs. Hill rushed off to find a Tilley lamp. I sat on the front bench with a grubby little Indian girl cuddled up to me and playing with my hands which, though sunburnt, were very white beside hers. She smelt like a little dog (!) but was a sweet little girl all the same. At the end of the meeting, the Indian who was leading it, again told the people who I was and why I had come to Bolivia and he prayed asking the Lord to bless me. One of the people asked for a special hymn for me. It was all about welcome and asking the Lord to be with me. It was a strange experience realising that these people to whom I had come, should be praying for **me.** The women were all wrapped in rugs over their many skirts and wore the typical felt hats of the region. In spite of the cold they wore only sandals on their feet. Afterwards they all came and gave me a firm, sticky handshake, and the women even hugged me.

Now I am back in my luxurious bed awaiting tomorrow's adventures.

...I forgot an important point. The customs officials' on the train had had orders not to touch the baggage of the English Señorita and, when they found I was with Mr. Hill, they all shook hands with me and smiled, evidently saying nice things in Spanish. Their orders came from a higher authority, but I guess the ultimate 'Higher Authority' had put it into their hearts. It was almost "red carpet" treatment.

21.10.57

"It's a great life if you don't weaken!" The Hills took me out to the Salt Lake of Uyuni. What an incredible place—a lake of salt eighty kilometres in each direction onto which we drove out. Mr. Hill's Jeep is, as he says, "a rattling good one." Five minutes is fun, an hour is an endurance test, and more is sheer agony! Later, Customs undid all my boxes (in front of an interested audience) but charged me nothing.

POTOSI
23.10.57

Of all the perilous journeys, yesterday's was the worst! I was scared stiff. The rail car ride was organised by Mr. Warder in La Paz and was a luxurious way of travel—a diesel coach with armchairs inside. It was quite comfortable, but it rattled along at speed and swayed from side to side; I felt as though I was in a washing machine. The Hill family travelled with me and I was so glad to have company. It took seven and a half hours and we went up to over 15,000 feet. All this was around bends which I wouldn't dare in an English train. I didn't mind if the precipice was on the outside of the bend and we tipped inwards, but the other side was awful. If ever I prayed on a journey, it was then. I hung on and shut my eyes. Anyway, the Lord got us safely to Potosí (14,000 feet) and I am very grateful. Dr. and Mrs. Hamilton met me and will take me tomorrow to Dr. and Mrs. Brown in Alcatuyo, my final destination.

I like Potosí. It is a colourful city of narrow streets, all of which seem to be going uphill. The women all wear full skirts of brightly coloured material, with blouses and shawls. Their hats are like the traditional Welsh hats, and most are white with satin ribbons.

This place is the most fascinating I have seen in all my travels, and it was worth the difficulties of the journey to get here. Maybe the novelty will wear off, but at the moment, it really feels like an exciting foreign land.

Dr. and Mrs. Hamilton are looking after me splendidly. They are so afraid I shall get in a draught or something, and I'm having quite a job to persuade them that I am a really tough young person. Dr. Hamilton keeps offering me aspirin or coramine against the altitude, but I feel as fit as a fiddle! I've felt no effect of the altitude except that I do tire quickly. I'm sure this is an answer to prayer as everyone seems to think I should be in a state of collapse!

The railcar was at the railway's expense and the Hamiltons say it has never been known before. The Lord provided for me so wonderfully yet again.

3

Alcatuyo

OCTOBER 1957

I have been in Bolivia for just one week. I can hardly believe it! Alcatuyo is quite nice. It is a country village much more pleasing than the town of Uyuni which was my first sight of Bolivia. There are fields surrounded by stone walls, though nothing much seems to be growing. The paths between the walls are stony and only wide enough for a laden donkey. There are very few trees. All around are magnificent mountain ranges. At sunset they are tinted in gorgeous shades of pink, orange, purple and deep blue; and then later as the sky darkens, myriads of stars twinkle through the clear night air.

I am at present the guest of Dr. and Mrs. Brown (Roger and Dell) and their house is really very attractive. Basically, it is built of adobes like the Indian houses but they have it plastered and whitewashed, and it has tiles on the roof like the houses in town. It is really as comfortable as one can be in the country, but with no modern conveniences. I have a room in a separate building which also includes the surgery. My luggage boxes, covered with plastic curtaining, serve as furniture; the pictures on the wall are tea towels, and, with a bed and some bits of furniture belonging to the Browns, I am content with my lot. I do long, though, for a drink of cold water! It just isn't the same after it has been boiled. Dr. and

Mrs. Brown work very hard and are tired. I can see the need for more workers, especially men—and I am only a girl!

I do wish you could look in on our doings! Today, for instance, is "Todos Santos" (All Saint's Day) and, for the Indians, it is a very important fiesta. They drink chicha copiously (a horrible looking brown, turbid, fermented liquid) and call up the spirits of any family members who have died during the year. All this is a dreadful temptation to the Christians whose families expect them to join in, so the missionaries try to provide other things for them to do. We went into a village called Puna this morning and met some of the Indian Christians there. I wish you could meet Cerilo, an old man with such a radiant face. He greeted me with a very firm handshake and a pat on my shoulder. There were two or three younger men in the group, and a blind man who reads Braille (in Spanish of course) and is led about by a grubby little lad of about three years old. a few women and children completed the company. We had a meeting with them and sang some hymns. Dr. Brown preached about what happens after death since this is uppermost in their minds during these days, and we sang the well known hymn, "Up from the grave He arose" like this:

Causarimpunña Señor,
Tucuy atiniyoj Salvador
Wicharimun sepulturamantaka
Wañuyta atipaj causarimpurka,
Señorniy, causanña,
Salvadorniy causashan.

This evening we had another meeting in Alcatuyo itself. The little hall is very unpretentious so that the Indians will feel at home. The seats are rough benches or even just planks laid across boxes and late-comers have to sit on the steps. In general, the men sit on one side and the women on the other. The women tend to come in late and, regardless of the preaching, they brightly and politely greet everyone else individually before they sit down. "Buenas noches...Buenas noches...Buenas noches!" It must be frustrating for Roger as he is preaching. It is interesting to see their culture pattern, so different from our own and yet with a real dignity about it. Their clothing is of a coarse brown material, hand spun and hand woven from the wool of their own sheep or llamas. Their hats (which men, women and children wear constantly) are of a natural coloured felt and usually very dirty. I suspect that they rarely, if ever, wash or comb their hair; some of the women's long thick plaits look terribly tangled. In spite of their unkempt condition, some of them truly love the Lord, and they enjoy coming to the meetings even though their understanding is limited.

The blind man was at the meeting again; I've learned that his name is Fructoso. The little lad who leads him around was dressed in a cut-down thick jumper and a bit of cotton material tied round his middle; a runny nose completed the picture. By the way, babies don't wear nappies (diapers to my American friends) or anything like that. Why bother? They only get dirty!

What problems can arise with missionaries' children! I have been interested in little Ruthie here. She is five and her older brother and sister are far away in boarding school in Cochabamba. Ruthie plays with the Indian children and is a real little Indian herself, speaking Quechua fluently; she obviously thinks in that language as she cannot always translate into English. She carries her doll and all her possessions in a cloth on her back and she eats with her fingers; she does everything Indian fashion. She is a lovely little girl.

Travelling in the car still terrifies me! Many of the roads are dreadfully dangerous, and there are always little black hairy pigs, dogs and chickens wandering all over the road. Sometimes we give a playful push with the car to a lazy donkey that won't get out of the way. Herds of llamas run in front of the car instead of getting out of the way, and as we bounce over boulders and drive through ditches or over precarious bridges, I lose any inclination to drive out here.

After an early breakfast on Sundays, Dell sings hymns over the loudspeaker to announce that the meeting is about to begin. There are no clocks in Indian homes; they get up when the sun comes up and the day has had time to warm up a bit. After the meeting in Alcatuyo, off we go to Puna for the day. It is market day in Puna and the Indian women squat around on the roadside with their wares spread in front of them while the men lounge around in groups talking. Some fruit and vegetables are on sale, especially potatoes, oka (another kind of potato), corn and broad beans. Other women sell bread (made of peanuts!), dye for their clothes, wooden spoons, decorated enamel plates and mugs. By far the most important merchandise is the coca leaf. There are bales and bales of coca, sold by handfuls, while others sell a kind of grey ash which they use to chew with the coca to help extract the drug, cocaine. Coca smells dreadful and the dirty green juice on the teeth looks quite revolting. The effect on the users is stupefaction, but the Browns tell me that they use it to numb the stomach against the pangs of hunger!

A good crowd gathers to listen as Roger preaches in the plaza and Dell sings. Some will stand and listen for a long time. The afternoon, which takes place in the home of a Christian, is taking quite a lot of getting used to. Children run in and out and the women breastfeed their babies openly; it becomes quite difficult to ignore the distractions and concentrate. I am trying to learn Spanish, but there is no one here for me to converse with. It is a strange feeling to hear laughter in conversation and occasionally the word, "Señorita" only to know that they are talking about me!

SUNDAY
10.11.57

A lovely day—the blind man was baptised in the river at Puna.

Sunday began as usual with Mrs. Brown singing to call folk to the meeting; the little room was crowded and we had a grand time. Then with a truckload of Indians we set off to Puna, about half an hour's journey over a reasonable road (apart from boulders, pigs, donkeys and chickens!). Other Christians from nearby villages joined us at the river bank and we were quite a crowd. It was difficult to find enough water, but eventually a pool was found (very dirty water) and Dr. Brown led Fructoso into the water and baptised him. His affirmation of faith was a joy to hear even though I didn't understand what he said. He has been so excited and counting the days. His wife came to see the baptism, though until now she has been very antagonistic. The meeting afterwards was lovely as we simply remembered the Lord in the "Breaking of Bread." Fructoso prayed, bubbling over with the joy of the Lord. The next item was a cup of tea all round. Fortunately the Indians like tea the way I, too, like it: with sugar but no milk; so out came the Primus stove and kettle and we had tea and bread. The bread is in flat round cakes, dry and unsalted, and the only way to make it palatable is to dunk it in the tea. No butter and jam here! I was struck by the very real happiness of the believers. It is so strange listening to conversation interspersed with laughter and not understanding, but I'm getting familiar with the hymns.

The Browns are very concerned about Juana, a Christian lady with a tuberculous spine. Over a trivial matter, a family row has sprung up and they all say it is because Juana is an "evangelista." Her father-in-law threatens to kill her and to kill the Browns if they go near her. Her father says, "Let her die," and her husband is too scared to stand up for her. Dr. Brown still goes (while her husband keeps watch) to give her injections and Mrs. Brown takes her food. We don't know what will happen. The stress has undermined her already poor health and she may soon die. That, they would say, is judgement on her because she is a Christian. I wonder if my faith would stand that kind of strain—would yours? For these people it is such a costly thing to be a Christian. They have none of the props that we have such as devotional books and magazines or big meetings and conferences. They haven't even got the whole Bible yet and not many can read anyway. I am beginning to realise how much I have leaned on these things.

You would laugh at me at bedtime! I stagger forth from the Brown's house to my own little room on the far side of the property with a kettle of boiling water, various items tucked under my arm, and my Tilley lamp swinging (I have not yet mastered the art of lighting it so Roger does that for me).

(Looking back now, from the turn of the millennium, I am amazed that I dared to sleep over there alone and that I was never molested by the Indians who lived around. It didn't occur to me at the time and I was blissful in my ignorance of what could have happened and has been known to happen to others. The Lord must have watched over me in answer to the many prayers of folk at home, and I am everlastingly grateful to them.)

This little room is my castle and I love it. We are supposed to be above the insect line but little black beetles drop out of the rafters landing on their backs with a cracking sound, and after a few frantic kicks, they roll on to their tummies and walk off. Moths fly around me, and one evening a frog came to join me. Lizards race around outside and last night some live thing was having a merry time in my wastepaper basket. A bird flew in and sat on the beams. Having visions of a mess to clear up, I had to call the long-suffering Roger to capture it and set it free. The birds here are very pretty, quite small but all colours, almost like budgerigars, and there are humming-birds too. I'm afraid I talk to these creatures: I said to the frog, "Alright my lad, I can't do anything about you tonight, but just wait till I get the broom out in the morning!"

One day we went to preach at a fair in a place called Pacasi. Fairs or "fiestas" are held in honour of a local "saint," and the drinking and dancing goes on for several days. As we arrived at the corner of the plaza, my first reaction was of pleasure. I was amazed at the colourful scene as the crowds of people were all dressed in their very best and had paper flowers in their hats. They use different colours from our favourites, predominantly pinks, purples, greens and turquoise, while blue and yellow are rarely seen. All around the plaza, women were sitting with their colourful wares spread out in front of them…food, sweets, clothes.

All seemed harmless and happy, but gradually I became aware of a dreadful discordant noise as five bands approached. Each was playing a different tune and was preceded by crazy, drunken men jigging about and surrounded by stupefied men and women dancing. How sad it was to see tiny babies on the backs of some of these women, their little heads lolling to the beat of the music. The Indians use drums, and pipes consisting of reeds differing in length and tied together. They play them by blowing across the top. After an hour or so of this, the music was just banging through my head till I felt like screaming for it to stop. Some men danced out of the village church with enormous silver wings tied to their backs. Then came the highlight of the occasion when the saint was carried shoulder high round the plaza. The "saint" was a gaudy, tinselly figure, standing about three feet high, with a mask-like face and carrying a cross. What a terrible travesty of anything even approaching the truth of the gospel! The people all removed their hats in respect, revealing a sea of tousled jet black hair. It looked so strange and the atmosphere was sinister. This was a test for the few Christians. The little group were conspicuous as they stood there, resolute, with their hats on; it needed courage not to remove them. In the midst of it all was the priest, swept along, jostled and harassed and not looking at all happy. Poor souls—what slaves they are to ignorance and really to Satan himself! Suddenly Ruthie Brown clasped my hand and said, "I'm frightened." In reassuring her I realised that I was frightened too; one could almost feel the power of evil palpating in the air. On the way home a young man who has been attending meetings for a few weeks asked to buy a

Quechua New Testament. I remembered he had kept his hat on as the "saint" went by. Perhaps something of the reality of Christ and the way of salvation has begun to dawn on him. We do pray so. Things are certainly happening here, but it is a slow plod.

~~~~~~~~~~~~~~~~~~~~~~

I thought you might like to know something of how the children here on the altiplano of Bolivia live. In the towns most of them live in ramshackle dirty houses, but they go to school every day. They have to wear white overalls over their clothes; a good idea as this covers the dirt underneath, but the white doesn't stay white for very long, as you can imagine. I am living in the country though, so I know most about the Indian children. When they are tiny babies they are tightly bound to keep them from wriggling around. A piece of cloth about three inches wide is wound 'round and 'round them, pinning their arms and legs down in the belief that this helps them to grow straight while they are carried in a kind of rug, called a manta, on their mother's backs. They are carried like this until they are about 3 years old, or until they are displaced by another baby coming into the family. The babies wear knitted hats with earflaps but as they get a bit older they have little round felt hats with brims. The hats always look quite out of proportion on tiny heads sticking out of the top of the manta!

I'm sure you would find Indian clothes horribly uncomfortable. The wool comes from their own sheep or llamas, and they make them entirely by themselves. First of all the women and girls spin the wool on a thing called a pushka, which looks rather like a top and spins like one on the end of the thread. It looks so easy but I can't do it at all and the thread always breaks when I try. I'm so frustrated as even the little girls can do it! When it is spun they weave it on very primitive looms, and then the cloth is made up into clothes. These are all brown or black (most sheep are black here) so are very drab, but they do weave some lovely coloured threads into the borders or else stitch brightly coloured braid along
~~~~~~~~~~~~~~~~~~~~~~

the edges. Round their waists they wear brightly coloured and woven belts and tuck all their personal belongings into this. Over the dress they have another piece of material which I can't quite make out. It seems to go halfway round them and tucks in to form a sort of pouch in which they keep more treasures. All is pinned together with a large pin that has a spoon shape at one end (useful for eating) and the sharp end can be used for poking things, digging wax out of their ears etc. Felt hats are also made of llama wool.

You don't really need a hankie as the hem of the skirt serves very well for this purpose. Underwear isn't worn so the toilet is just to squat wherever you happen to be! Going to bed is easy as all you need to do is take off your hat, and your shoes if you have any, and stretch out on the sheepskin spread out on a mud platform which serves as a bed. An extra blanket covers you for the freezing cold night. For supper you might have a bowl of highly seasoned soup with some meat and potatoes or wheat in it, or perhaps some beans and sweet corn. You would have only one meal a day and for the rest a little bag of dried corn (chicken feed to us!) would keep the pangs of hunger at bay.

From the age of about four the children have to mind the pigs, sheep and donkeys. A girlie of about eight years old will take a whole flock of sheep out to find pasture for them, a difficult job on these arid mountains. There is no grass here and she may have to walk miles to find some scrub. She may even have to climb the occasional tree to cut down leaves for the sheep to eat. All the time she carries her pushka and is spinning. Most of these children have never heard of the Lord Jesus. They are afraid of spirits and are taught to worship the "saints" which are idols really. They know little of God, nothing of prayer, and have never heard that the Lord Jesus loves them and died for them.

4

Two and a Half Miles High

It became my first consideration to learn Spanish well and, as Alcatuyo is an entirely Quechua speaking area, it was suggested that I should accept the invitation of Dr. and Mrs. P. Hamilton to be with them in the city of Potosí for a time.

DECEMBER 1957

So here I am in Potosí again. I was here for a few days at the end of my train journey when I first came to Bolivia, and it was the Hamiltons who cared for me and took me out to Alcatuyo. By a real miracle, a room became available adjacent to their flat. It had been refused them on several previous occasions but, in answer to their prayers, I was able to move in. Potosí is a remarkable city. It sits 14,000 feet up in the Andes mountains with Mt. Potosí towering another 3,000 feet above it. The mountain is riddled with mines, which produce only tin now, though it was once rich with silver. The mountain is streaked with different coloured minerals with a Catholic shrine on top. The city has narrow streets (most of which seem to go uphill!) with not much pavement. In some places you need to flatten yourself against a wall when a truck passes. On each crossing there is a busy policeman importantly blowing a whistle each time a car appears but seeming uncertain as to which way he wants it to go!

There are three distinct classes of people here: the Indians, who perhaps come in from the country for a day; the proud "Gente" descended from the Spanish, with more or less a European style of dress; and, in between, the half-caste Cholos who are the small shopkeepers, miners and builders. The Chola dress is distinctive, with very full skirts covering many petticoats, colourful fringed mantas (shawls) and high wide-brimmed hats. Houses are in keeping with the status of the family, from some very nice homes of the Gente to the very humble dwellings of the Cholos. In Spanish fashion, they are built around a courtyard or "patio" and may be painted white or blue. The aspect is generally dingy, though a glimpse into a patio sometimes brings a nice surprise of unbelievably colourful flowers in paved courtyards, and fountains splash in some of them.

Let me take you to my home. In a street which runs alongside the market is a doorway where we find a dark little sweetshop, and behind the shop is an even darker little room where the owners of the shop live with their family. We pass through the shop and past the room (remembering to say "Buenos días" nicely as we pass) where we come out into a surprisingly pleasant patio with paving and four trees. These trees are a lifesaver for me as it is such a relief to see something green and growing. There are rooms all around the patio, and a long flight of stairs in the middle leads up to a wide balcony on all sides with rooms on two opposite sides. The Hamiltons live on the innermost side of this balcony, the Bolivian owners on the street side, and I have one of their rooms. I have double doors on to the balcony and, with the inside door locked, I can be independent. I have brilliant blue walls and an actual ceiling (also bright blue) so I don't have to worry about bugs dropping on me any more. They have lent me an enormous wardrobe with a full-length mirror, (luxury indeed!) a bed, table and chair. I have all my meals with the Hamiltons, (how wonderfully kind they are to me) but I have a Primus stove and kettle so I can brew my own tea while applying my mind to the task of learning Spanish. This room is my refuge. The electric light varies in intensity according to how many lights are in use, and sometimes it gives up altogether, but it is a great joy all the same. My big worry now is the dog downstairs—a horrid little dachshund—and we have taken a mutual dislike to each other. I dare not go downstairs unaccompanied if she is in the patio.

On Thursday I went to a meeting with Mrs. Hamilton. It was in Quechua in a small hall, way up in the Indian part of the city. The hall was full and Mrs. Hamilton was the speaker. At one point the women put up their hands and I wondered vaguely why. Mrs. Hamilton suddenly spotted me and she just laughed and laughed! Then she came over to me and patted my shoulder affectionately and explained (in English) that she had asked who would like to go to heaven. Apparently the only one who didn't want to go there was the new missionary! Last Saturday I spoke in Spanish for a minute or two and next week, I have ten whole minutes—what a terrifying thought!

Today I went to a Sunday School recitation rehearsal in preparation for Christmas. The activities didn't involve me too much, so I began idly drawing the scene. Before I knew it, I found I had provided a counter-attraction and had children all over me!

Many of you have asked what I do all day. Well, I eat, learn Spanish, have Spanish lessons and Spanish conversations, (with Lucia who comes to chat with me; I try to tell her about some of my photographs) I go to meetings with the Hamiltons, attend more meetings, and I visit the Post Office whenever a mail train comes in. Dr. and Mrs. Hamilton feed me too well: they say they believe in two hourly feeds. The bread is horribly dry and uninteresting, (Mrs. Brown made her own bread and it was lovely) and I am being introduced to many new vegetables and fruit. All salad and fruit has to be soaked for a time in potassium permanganate to avoid typhoid fever; we get imported powdered milk and all water has to be well boiled.

It is summertime at the moment and the beginning of the rainy season. From early morning it is hot. I sit outside to study in a summer dress with my Jamaican straw hat, but by 5 p.m. a cold wind springs up. As the sun goes down it becomes bitterly cold and on go the winter woollies. There hasn't been much rain yet, but we have had two violent hailstorms.

We don't celebrate Christmas here in Potosí because there is so much idolatry in the Roman Catholic festival, but we do make a big splash at the New Year with Sunday School prize givings and similar activities. For us, though, what joy it is to remember again the birth of the Babe who has changed our lives completely, and to go on from there to remember His life and death, His resurrection, and to eagerly anticipate His return. How amazing it is that such a One could care for each one of us individually. I have continually proved His care so much in all my affairs here in Bolivia, I just cannot cease to be amazed at the wonder of it! I am reminded of the headings of an address by Dr. Stephen Short given to nurses at Westminster Hospital—

Q1. Why should I bother about religion?

Q2. Why should I bother about Christianity?

Q3. Why should I bother about Christ?

Answer: Because He bothered so much about me.

~~~~~~~~~~~

Just before Christmas I had a new experience: Dr. Hamilton took me to the Police Station! We tried three times before anyone condescended to notice that we were there. They asked all kinds of questions about me such as, "Are you married?...single?...how many children?!" Then I was finger-printed—all ten fingers twice,
~~~~~~~~~~~

the thumb and forefinger of each hand twice more. I really began to feel like a convict when I was photographed holding a number across my chest! It was a dreadful photo, but at least I am nearer to getting the official documents necessary to reside as a stranger in this very strange land.

The Browns invited me to spend Christmas with them back in Alcatuyo; they came to collect me. Meryl and Roger were home from school, and one of their teachers had come too so it was quite a party. The teacher and I shared my old room, and we talked well into the night as I listened to her tales of missionaries' children at school. Christmas Day was a lovely family time. Amazingly, we lit on the Queen's speech in the middle of a Portuguese programme on the battery radio! Homesickness reared its unhappy head again!

I experienced my first earthquake in Alcatuyo. We were sitting at the table when it began to move. The light was swinging and I felt as though I was back on board ship. Mrs. Brown said, "Is it me or is this an earthquake?" We hurried outside but it didn't last long. We didn't hear of any damage, although in Potosí Dr. Hamilton had to treat some people for shock.

On Christmas night the rainy season arrived with a vengeance! We awoke to the noise of ominous pattering and sploshing and to find our beds slowly getting soggy. This is nothing unusual in Bolivia but it was my first experience—the Browns proudly say that they have "running water in every room" and it is just about true! We scrambled around in the dark moving our beds to the driest spot and shrieked as our bare feet found the puddles on the floor. Great fun!

The next day I was faced with the problem of getting back to Potosí as it was doubtful if the "gondola" (a ramshackle yellow bus) would run. It was decided that I would have to risk getting a lorry. (P.S. I get teased for talking about "lorries." To New

Zealanders and Americans they are "trucks," and to Bolivians "camiones." I'll use one or other of those words from now on.) Going by truck means a long, long wait but eventually, just before lunch, five were seen travelling across the pampa together. Apparently they travel together in bad weather in order to help one another if someone gets stuck. I had time just to gulp a plate of soup, and then Dr. Brown took me out to the road to wait until the trucks appeared. The first one to arrive was bright yellow. When the driver agreed to take me I was able to clamber up into the cab with him and his wife and begin to enjoy seeing things from an unusual angle. But…it was a stop-start experience; after about 5 minutes we stopped to refill the gasoline tank (hereafter petrol=gasoline=gas. We use all three terms) and shortly after to help another truck in trouble. Each start meant a considerable and noisy cranking until the engine jumped into life and off we went. I was determined to sit back and enjoy the situation. I wasn't very keen about these precipitous roads, deep with mud, but the driver seemed careful enough. It wasn't long before we stopped at a hotel (you should have seen it!) where everyone went in for lunch.

Dell Brown had given me some sandwiches and, having finished them, I soon began to wish we could get going again. Forlorn hope—we were there for 3½ hours! My "paciencia" (patience) was sorely tried. An Indian boy came and tried talking to me. I watched the fun on one of the other trucks as they set about unloading a few bags of flour which they had packed at the bottom, under drums of gasoline! It provided nearly two hours of entertainment as they struggled to take about a dozen drums of gas off, and then load them back on, the truck. I had noticed two very rascally looking men wandering around; both were very fat, unshaven and with long dark moustaches. One was in a corduroy suit and battered trilby and the other wore a sweater and beret. They looked truly sinister and I avoided catching their eye, hoping they wouldn't come near me.

Eventually a young man came over to me and, with much gesticulating, he indicated that I was to transfer to another of the trucks which would be going first. I moved over and settled myself in the cab, glad to be on the move at last and wondering who the driver might be. Imagine my horror when the two rascally men got in, one on either side of me, squashing me between them! I had to laugh at myself: Betty—who scorns to hitchhike in England—settled between two greasy fat men in a truck in this wildest of countries. However, I must put on record that they were the essence of courtesy; one went to sleep and the other concentrated on driving, for which two blessings I was profoundly thankful. The journey wasn't too bad. The heavy truck held the road well, the driver was careful and I got safely back to Potosí, thrilled to be there, as one can sometimes get stuck for weeks by the rain.

I noticed again how enormous are the cacti which grow around here (much taller than a man) and the lovely red flowers they have at the top. The llamas are fascinating too; some have little bits of coloured wool in their ears, presumably as a means of identification, and they are so dignified, yet quaint. Thunderstorms are very heavy and I'm told this is because of the mineral content of the mountains around; often people are struck by lightning. There is a lot of superstition about lightning so that to be struck shows you have been meddling with the devil, and if you walk over a piece of ground which has previously been struck, you will become ill. It is interesting that in the village of Pacasi, where gum trees have been introduced, thunderstorms and hailstorms seem to skirt the village.

I am still concentrating on learning Spanish. I must get really familiar with it so that I can get the right words without thinking. Theoretically, I can say a lot, but it takes me ages to arrange my thoughts and conversation becomes tedious. I still rush off to the Post Office when the train comes in (giving them a bit of time to sort the mail!). I can cope with buying stamps and doing some shopping, but the thought of bargaining in the market still terrifies me.

~~~~~~~~~~~~~~

Early in the New Year we did a trip to Pacasi to take the prizes for Sunday School. Much preparation was required as we had to take bedding, food and cooking utensils. Eventually everything was stowed in the camioneta (a light truck—in this case a blue Dodge) and we set out in the rain. Oh the rain! The road was deep in mud and I was not very happy as we slithered round the bends. As we progressed the road got worse, and so did the rain. Water was rushing down the mountainside forming a purple stream on one side of the road and yellow on the other, then it would change to pink and green, all depending on the minerals in the locality. We crossed several fast rivers: one I remember particularly was wide and fast but we did not know how deep it was. As we drew up on one bank, the gondola (local bus) drew up on the other side and we surveyed each other with interest. The danger is not only in the depth of the river but in the possibility of boulders breaking the axle of the car. Dr. Hamilton decided to watch while the gondola went through as it was a much higher vehicle than ours and it would give us some idea of whether we could get across. After a while a man jumped out of the gondola and walked to the water's edge. He took off his shoes and rolled his trouser legs up, then he changed his mind and took his trousers right off—at least he was wearing underpants! The water came up to his thighs but he did ascertain that there were no boulders in the way. The driver of the gondola lifted the bonnet, covered the engine with his coat and drove safely through. Dr. Hamilton decided to do the same and to remove the fan belt as well as cover the engine. We prayed earnestly for safety and then drove carefully through. You can imagine that we stopped to thank the Lord on the other side; I was so relieved that I could hardly speak. I had been scared! On arrival in Pacasi we had to put the house in order and clean things up as it had not been occupied for some time. That night it contin-
~~~~~~~~~~~~~~

ued to pour with rain and I was thankful to be dry, though there were ominous drippings in other parts of my little room.

On Sunday morning it was still raining and we were afraid folk would not venture out. They did arrive eventually, however, and some had waded through rivers. It was Sunday School time first and, under the guidance of a young Indian called Feliciano, the children sang choruses and recited long passages from the Bible. The Indians are so different from the townsfolk, I just love them. Imagine rows of children (especially well-behaved for the occasion) sitting on benches, boys on one side and girls on the other, ragged in the extreme. Some of their homespun clothes seemed to be darns joined together. Most of the children were barefoot, though a few had sandals made out of old motor tyres. The boys' black hair is usually a shaggy mop while most of the girls have untidy plaits. The boys wear ponchos and the girls wear homespun mantas wrapped around them. Their merry brown faces appealed to me so much and they laughed as I tried to mimic Quechua phrases.

Have you ever seen a child who has never possessed *anything* receive a toy? It is such a joy. One little girl was given a doll, and in a trice her manta was off and the "baby" lovingly wrapped in it and slung on her back. These children were so thrilled with the smallest gifts; tears came to my eyes as I watched them. I took some photos after Sunday School but found the Indians very hesitant about posing for me. Popular belief has it that the click of the camera takes their soul away. Five Indian men, each carrying a special stick, came through the gate in single file (truly "Indian file") and I learned that they were the village chiefs. After they had talked with Dr. Hamilton, they were very pleased to have their photo taken, but instead of grouping themselves sensibly, they insisted on standing solemnly in a row; then they marched solemnly out of the gate, still in single file. The leader had a silver stick indicating that he was the headman. It was quite a weird performance; I was amused when I learned how important they were because I had shooed them out of the way while I was photographing the children. I should have treated them with greater respect!

After the next meeting it was so late and we were all so hungry that Mrs. Hamilton decided to provide bread and coffee all around, an ample lunch for the Indians who have their main meal at night. Indian bread is like sawdust but dipping it in the coffee as the Indians do wasn't too bad. We went back into the house for what was left of the afternoon, and it was then that Dr. Hamilton discovered a very dead rat in the middle of a cushion! Further investigation revealed the mother and her babies (very dead too) in the upholstered arm of the wicker chair in which I was sitting! They fell on the floor as I moved! No wonder the house had a horrible smell when we arrived! What a joy it was in the evening to hear these Indian folk singing praises to the Lord; many of them really had their hearts in it. The Lord certainly changes lives, a fact which is borne out by the number of sullen coca-chewing men and women who have become delightful Christians.

On Monday a long queue of patients sat outside the door waiting to see Dr. Hamilton. Some were genuinely ill while others were regular attenders who just seem to like it. I had a grand time filling capsules, stirring mixtures and mixing ointments. In the sunshine Pacasi is lovely and the view from the house across the village to the mountains is magnificent. I went for a walk and sat by a stream just watching the clear water sparkling among the boulders, while some children observed me with interest. The journey back to Potosí next day was a complete contrast to the horrible journey out. The sun shone and it was really hot as we picnicked beside a little waterfall. I couldn't resist dabbling my toes in the water and scrambling among the rocks.

Circumstances have been rather uncertain. Dr. and Mrs. Hamilton are soon off on furlough to the U.S. and, as it is not proper (or safe) for a Señorita to live alone, I must move and accept the hospitality of some other kind missionaries. Mr. and Mrs. Randall

(Bert and Eileen) of Tupiza have invited me to join them and I expect to be travelling there in the next week or two. I'm looking forward to Tupiza; the altitude is less (about 9,800 feet) and the climate correspondingly better, so perhaps I shall have a little more energy to get on with things. The winter is approaching and it will be very cold indeed here in Potosí, so I am not too bothered about moving on. I would value prayer as I go on learning Spanish. It needs "grace of continuance" and the tempter has such good ideas about what might be more fun and still very useful!

I'm sorry to leave the church here in Potosí. There are between forty and fifty baptised believers. I do wish you could see them—the men on one side of the hall, dressed in a motley collection of semi-European garments, and the women on the other side looking for all the world like a row of witches in their tall hats and shawls; but the Lord being in their hearts and shows in their faces. The hall is packed for meetings and Sunday school (it holds over one hundred). It is super to see so many young men who are interested. There is much hope for the future if they will only "wholly follow the Lord."

Again I feel the need for prayer as I leave for Tupiza; once again I shall be leaving all that has become familiar to me.

5

Too Many Peaches

TUPIZA, MARCH 1958

My first few days at Tupiza cannot be called a howling success! I have spent the best part of two days in bed suffering from a surfeit of peaches. After the barrenness of Potosí, fruit is abundant here and a visit to a peach orchard was my undoing! I'm on the mend though and hope to be back to normal tomorrow.

I left Potosí at 6 p.m. last Thursday, amazed at the number of friends I have acquired in my three months there; a good crowd came to see me off on the train. There were Dr. and Mrs. Hamilton of course, Miss Seary (of the Evangelical Union of South America), Carlos, one of the boys from the house where I lived, Lucía, Louisa, Mercedes, and even my best boyfriend Benjamín, a lovely little chap of three years old whom I am sure will be absolutely devastating when he grows up!

It seems extravagant that a missionary should travel in a First Class sleeping compartment, but I assure you that for a 22-hour journey in Bolivia it is no luxury! Even travelling in this way is wearying, hot and dirty. I had as companion in my "camarote" a grubby Bolivian woman with a little girl. The child spat grape skins all over the floor…so much for First Class! I watched the mountains go by for a while, then demolished the sandwiches Mrs. Hamilton had supplied and retired to bed. My bunk was the top one and since the ladder was behind a pile of luggage, there was nothing for it but to clamber up without it; anyway, the luggage collapsed beneath me, making it easy to get the ladder out! I have become hardened now to the hair-raising bends and precipices of the railways and roads here. I just watch with interest and think, "Surely we are not going round there—youch! We are!" I slept like a baby while we wound around the mountains in the dark. I woke at 2 a.m. to find we were at Río Mulatos. There, our coach was to be joined to the main La Paz-Buenos Aires train. We were there so long I thought we must have been forgotten. I went to sleep again and woke up at 7 a.m. in Uyuni where my companions left me. Uyuni is the place where I had spent my first two or three days in Bolivia.

The morning was monotonous and the scenery all alike as we ambled across an immense, sandy, scrubby plateau (the Altiplano) with enormous sand dunes, wind-rippled and resembling golf bunkers; on both sides mountains rose in the distance. Occasionally we passed little clusters of houses with men and women lounging at the doors and the children playing together. I wondered many, many times if anyone had ever told them of Christ and His redeeming love for them. What can life hold for them apart from Him? No wonder they drink and chew coca and live immorally—there is nothing else to do. I think it would drive me quite mad to live in such a wilderness; they are probably unaware that there is anything better in this world. I think we have much to be thankful for in the homes into which we were born.

At 11 a.m. we arrived at Atocha—a string of sun-baked mud houses at the edge of a wide river bed and not a tree in sight. Again I wondered if anyone had preached, "Christ and Him crucified" and risen, there. (Later I learned that there are believers in Atocha).

I was leaning out of the window pondering these things when I was accosted by a tall, dark and handsome young man who had been walking up and down outside. "Excuse me, but have I not seen you with Dr. Hamilton?" He proved to be a Bolivian, studying at the Methodist College in Buenos Aires. He had been to talk with Dr. Hamilton on several occasions and I remember hearing about him but had not met him. He spoke a little English so, between us, we got along quite well. As the train started and he needed to jump on, he invited me to lunch in the dining car with himself and his cousin. I was glad to have help in manoeuvring my way through lunch; the things we ate (I thought this might have been the reason for my upset soon after I arrived, but Mr. Randall has succumbed today so it can't have been)! The first course was salad; this was a bit tricky as I had been told never to eat salad on trains, but I was with Bolivians and had to do as they did. I skipped the lettuce and trusted the Lord and my typhoid injection for the rest. Next there came a greasy soup with all manner of things floating in it, then chicken and rice. That, I thought, would be the end of the meat courses, but no, we went on to some kind of meat and butter beans, and finally stewed fruit and coffee. The young man's cousin was a joy. She proved to be a good bit older, a Bolivian lady who had lived in England for thirty years and was revisiting Bolivia. I gathered that her husband is English and they live in Devon. We had a great time talking (in English) about the places we both knew…Torquay, Dartmouth, etc. It was a real tonic as even the missionaries here seem to be mainly from New Zealand or the U.S.A. and don't know these places.

After lunch I returned to my camarote for a rest. The scenery had begun to change and for miles we followed the broad river bed, the little stream flowing along it doing little credit to the fact that the rainy season is barely over. The landscape got gradually greener with trees and with sweet corn growing in the fields. Just before Tupiza I was amazed to hear my name called from outside the train window! I leaned out and there, leaning out of the next window, was my handsome friend! He gave me his card and hoped I would write, a forlorn hope I'm afraid. At last we ambled, with much whistle blowing and children running alongside and jumping on the train, into Tupiza station where Mr. and Mrs. Randall and Paul (aged ten and the youngest of three) were there to meet me.

Tupiza (pronounced Too-pee-sa) is more what I imagined a South American town to be. The streets are mainly just sandy dirt, though there are pavements in places, and there are some trees including tropical palms already dry and brown even though the rains are only just over. Horseback seems to be a common method of transport. At an altitude of 10,000 feet, it is intensely hot and I am learning the value of a siesta in the afternoon; I'm so glad I am not in the jungle; it must be unbearable. On Saturday we visited an old lady out in the country and she loaded us with peaches and dahlias from her garden. (I ate far too many of the peaches and that is probably why I suffered so badly.)

I have been given such a warm welcome here. The children eye me up and down and shyly finger my clothes. I wish I could talk to them easily and fluently. They wear lighter clothes here because of the heat; the men in trousers and shirt and the women in summer dresses. Some wear the Chola dress but I haven't seen any Quechua Indians.

We live above the Hall which is right opposite the station. A constant reminder of home and wartime is that station employees are reminded of the time by a siren; my insides turn over every time I hear it!

I've made friends with two girls who are missionaries with the Evangelical Union of South America and work in Vitichi. One is Canadian and the other American; they are great. We have so much in common. One of them, Mildred, is an examiner in Spanish for their mission and she is going to put my Spanish to the test. It will be good to know how I am doing, and I hope to visit Mildred and Milly from here.

Bolivia could well be called 'The Land of the Crooked Cross,' for I have noticed in my travels that on so many mountain peaks there stands a large wooden cross, often at a rakish, irreverent angle. It is supposed to keep hail away from the crops, but its own crookedness can surely give little confidence. It merely serves to underline the crookedness of everything here like, for instance, the dealings of a man with his neighbour, the matrimonial affairs and religion. I can see one such cross from my window and it serves as a constant reminder of how, in this land, the things of God have been taken and twisted and mixed with idolatry so as to become quite unrecognisable. What a privilege it is to come here with the simple, unadulterated Bible message of the Gospel of salvation through faith in the Lord Jesus Christ. Easter time made me think and appreciate it again. The people are taught to believe that the Lord Jesus actually dies on Good Friday each year and that, from then until Easter Sunday, and the commemorating of the resurrection, God is actually dead! In that case He can't see what they are up to so it is a time of licentiousness and sin. Everyone takes special care to lock up their belongings during those few days. We gave away many copies of a booklet specially prepared for Easter by the Bible Society and called 'El Vive' (He Lives).

I like Tupiza. To begin with, the weather is grand—hot sunny days with cloudless skies, yet at night it is cold and a joy to cuddle up in bed. It is quite pleasant to sit in the shade of the trees in the plaza watching the world go by. The people are very clothes conscious and just live for dress, though their fashions are very out of date by our standards. They would look so out of place in London, but they think they are fine and pity us for having no dress sense at all! Personally I love the Chola dress; when they are really dressed up in their brilliant colours and finely pleated, very full skirts, with layers of petticoats underneath, they are splendid. It seems a pity that the younger generation is taking to European dress.

I have said that horses are used a lot here and it fascinates me to see them galloping into town. I still have hopes of learning to ride one day but I guess a more docile animal would suit me better. It will probably be a donkey!

The arrival of the daily train is fascinating too. There is intense excitement and the scene is so colourful—no drab suitcases here, but brilliant coloured bundles or "bultos." Personal goods are wrapped in woven stripy material and tied by the corners with two big knots on top with which they can be held and hauled up onto the back. A couple of chickens may be sitting on top. We sometimes buy bananas from the passengers on the train as they sell their wares out of the windows. Outside the station are little stalls where they sell fruit and rather questionable ice-cream and some lovely things called "umintas." These are made of minced sweet corn, cheese and cinnamon, wrapped in corn leaves and well boiled so they are safe to eat in spite of the grubby human hands that have prepared them. They taste lovely.

One thing that really makes me want to run home to mother is a horrid insect called a "binchuca." These unpleasant creatures are about half an inch or more across the flat body with legs spread-eagled all round. They are bloodsucking insects living especially in chicken runs but at night they come in determined to share my bed and my blood. I sleep in a circle of DDT but they climb up the walls, across the ceiling and drop on to the bed. All one knows about it usually are the black marks left on the sheets but I found a binchuca this morning so bloated with blood (presumably mine) that it looked like a fat grape and could hardly walk. The only way to catch them (they run very fast!) is to suddenly land a cotton wool ball on them from above. They get their legs entangled and you can squash them.

I am being introduced to new fruits. One is a tuna (prickly pear) which grows on a cactus, another is a chirimoya (custard apple) which is a greenish brown knobbly thing with white flesh and black pips scattered through it. It really does taste like apple and custard. You cut them in half and spoon the flesh out with a teaspoon.

Last week when we went over to the station, the train arrived with a military band playing, sitting on the roof of one of the coaches. It was very exciting. We had gone over to see Mr. and Mrs. Warder, the folk who were so very kind in organising my first journey from Antofagasta into Bolivia. Mr. Warder has a very high position in the Railway Company (British) here but I had never met him. It was good to be able to thank him for smoothing my journey so wonderfully; I liked Mr. and Mrs. Warder immensely. They invited me to stay with them in La Paz whenever I like. Mr. Warder says they have a good gaol there! The Randalls and I were very impressed with the mode of travel for important people. They had a whole coach to themselves with sitting room (nicely furnished with arm chairs and all), bedroom, kitchen and even a private cook! They were on their way to Buenos Aires for a holiday and would have to relinquish the posh coach at the Argentine frontier. Travelling in an ordinary camarote, but having meals with the Warders, were the couple who kindly let me use their house in Uyuni when I first arrived; I was glad to meet them too.

We made a trip one day to a village called Oploca and I enjoyed it tremendously. The Randalls have a Jeep truck and we bounced our way along the river bed which was still quite green after the rain but with barren reddish mountains on either side, the formation in some parts resembling ruined castles. It could almost be in England with its avenue of trees and whitewashed buildings. It used to be the farm of a big German mining company but Bolivia has taken control of the mines now. We bought some fresh butter and cheeses and are finding them quite a luxury. We visited a house made of mud and bare of furniture except for an ancient writing desk, where a Christian lady lived with six delightful children; the father was away working. I was most sorry for the dog; the poor thing's ribs were sticking out. They keep the dogs hungry here to make them fierce as guard dogs. The lady was sweet. She told us about a man who really seemed to be seeking the Lord and said, "He is outside working, wearing a red shirt." Shortly afterwards a man came in wearing a very red shirt. A Bolivian Christian who was with us, and Mr. Randall, read many verses from the Bible to him and explained as simply as possible the Way of Salvation through faith in the Lord Jesus Christ and His death for us and resurrection. How many miss the Way for its very simplicity! We knelt to pray and, there and then, he found peace and forgiveness in the Saviour. It was a worthwhile trip.

We went on to another Bolivian home for supper; a real contrast this, the home of one of the most important men of the village. We entered an attractive patio and were shown into a very big room which showed unmistakeable signs of departed glory. It could have been an English country mansion with its wood panelling and diamond paned windows. The furniture was sparse, enormous and grand, but very shabby. The dining room was similar and, although the people who live there are of the Cholo type, we had table and chairs, and the table was laid as nearly as possible as an English one might be. We had a delicious chicken soup and then I think they must have 'killed the fatted calf' as my piece of meat seemed about that size—only it was mutton! With that we had rice and carrot and afterwards the blackest of black coffee, something for which I am trying unsuccessfully to acquire a taste. I decided that everyone was very rude as I was the only one who carefully placed my knife and fork together. The tables turned on me though as I discovered that I was the rude one - it is polite here to leave the knife and fork at right angles to one another at a sort of 'twenty to four' angle on the plate. It isn't easy to do it deliberately after having different etiquette drilled into me since childhood. There are other points of etiquette to remember; for example, a guest must never be allowed to empty his plate before offering him more. However shall I behave when I come home on furlough? I shall need a course on culture and manners.

In the evening we had a meeting in the school, but there was no light. Candles were hastily brought from somewhere, but then they managed to rig up an electric light with one miserable little bulb. The meeting was lovely and folk were hiding outside the windows to listen. Coming home in the dark along the river bed was an adventure as the 'road' was pretty elusive, but we got home safely and my, was I tired!

Just briefly, I have started a children's meeting on Thursday mornings, as requested by some little girls, and it is a heavy strain on my Spanish. I've also started giving English lessons to a lady and her two boys in exchange for Spanish conversation...but more of this later.

~~~~~~~~~~~~~

We are so much in need of prayer here in Bolivia, and when I get to prayer myself I am overwhelmed and don't know where to start. A great cause for concern is the unrest in the country and we have no idea what will be the outcome. At present the P.O. and the Banks are on strike and there is some alarm as to whether the problem will be amicably settled or will lead to a major catastrophe.

A week or two ago I went on a day's trip into the country with Mr and Mrs. Randall and some Christians from Tupiza. We had a wonderful time and I enjoyed sitting on the back of the truck and trying to join in the conversation. We sang choruses as we drove along, much to the amazement of the folk we passed on foot or on horseback. The great thing in the country is to visit the schools, and on this trip we visited several. We also visited an old lady who is a Christian and lives alone...if you can call it alone when she is surrounded by innumerable donkeys, sheep and chickens! Paul made several attempts to fling his arms round the neck of one of the donkeys. The most interesting visit was to a village called San
~~~~~~~~~~~~~

Miguel, a place with quite a big school but absolutely buried in the country. The folk there were expecting us and we had a great welcome.

The school is a new building of adobes with no glass in the windows and the schoolmaster, who is a very new Christian, got all the children together so that we could give them Gospel leaflets and sing choruses to them. We taught them to sing a couple of hymns before Mr Randall talked to them briefly. They were cute little youngsters, ragged, dirty and mischievous, and they were thrilled to bits when I took their photograph. I talked for a while to the schoolmaster's wife, who also teaches, and the children were listening open-mouthed, probably wondering at my foreign looks and accent. We stayed on there for a meeting for adults in the evening, and the schoolroom was filled. Once again there was no electric light, but it was fascinating to watch the flickering candle light on earnest, listening faces. There and then the schoolmaster's wife came to the Lord, just as she was and in the presence of many people, and her husband was so pleased. Today, that same lady, Doña Carolina, came to visit us here in Tupiza and she is showing obvious signs of her new life in Christ. She bought a hymnbook and told us about the meetings they have and how her husband reads the Bible to them, and how she wants to start a Sunday School with the children (as if she didn't see enough of those children all the week!) She gets the children to sing the hymns we taught them when we visited even though they have no music and have to rely on their memories. What a tremendous influence this couple have for the Lord as they run the village school.

I have acquired quite a selection of English pupils; the bank manager's wife and two sons (dreadful boys!), the dentist's wife, son and daughter, and two teenage girls. They are, of course, all Roman Catholics and would not dream of coming to a meeting. I have stated my 'price' for the lessons, that if I teach them English they will then listen to me read a chapter from the Bible and correct my pronunciation, and today I read John's Gospel chapter 1. I read from the Catholic Bible and they followed in our version, this being to help refute their mistaken belief that ours is a different Bible. They often use this as an argument against the Gospel but in reality, although the wording may be slightly different, what the two versions say is essentially the same. I was amazed at the hush as I finished reading and they left quietly instead of bouncing out as they usually do. I do pray that their silence was because the words went home to them and not a silence of antagonism, and I do hope they return to hear more. I can't tell you what it meant to me to read that chapter to young, thinking Catholics who were obviously listening intently. It made me feel that I was really on the job. I had promised not to comment. They would probably not come if I did and I expect they will have to confess to the priest anyway. Perhaps he won't mind as I used the RC version.

Last Thursday was the day of 'First Communion' for many of the children here. I'm not surprised that the Catholic Church attracts children as they have this wonderful day of dressing up and receiving gifts from family and friends. They look so sweet; the little girls (aged around seven) are in long white dresses, veils, gloves and flowered head-dresses, and what little girl wouldn't want to walk up the aisle in a white dress or what big girl for that matter, like me?! The boys look a bit silly with a big white satin bow as an arm-band and they all carry elaborate candles. It is obviously the great day of their lives and one can hardly blame them. From their 'baptism' as babies, the Church of Rome, with all its idolatry, has claimed them as its own. They often say they must be faithful to the church but they know nothing of allegiance to Christ. It makes me shudder to see the idols they parade through the streets, tawdry plaster images, not in the name of a pagan religion, but in the name of God. They repeatedly pay the priest for peace of mind and for help for their deceased relatives, but they know nothing of the "peace which passes all understanding."

About ten little girls come along to my class each week, and sometimes they coax a school friend along for a couple of weeks; it lasts just until the child's parents hear about it. A 14-year old called Isabel often comes. Her mother (no longer living) was a Christian and her father, a very timid man, does not mind her coming. The main influence in her life is her grandparents and they are very averse to the Gospel. The girl is obviously interested and risks severe punishment to come. She often hides in case any of her neighbours should look in the door and catch a glimpse of her. It would be such a joy if she were to come to the Lord.

A converted priest is here in Tupiza at the moment. He is a good Gospel preacher and on previous visits he has led people to the Lord. We are not sure how long he will be here but he is a great help in the preaching as, at the moment, Mr Randall is away on a trip. I was expecting to be alone while they were away but, after all, Mrs. Randall has stayed with me.

We hear there are some new recruits for Bolivia coming soon. They certainly stand in need of prayer for the Lord's help in their preparations and that He might open up the way for them very soon.

Prayer is the mightiest weapon we can find,
    Prayer makes us patient, understanding, kind,
Leads us to right decisions, clears the mind,
    Prayer changes things.

(Source unknown)

6
Excitement in La Paz

AUGUST 1958

I am having a really adventurous time at the moment. It all began with my being ill! I had a badly infected throat twice, then measles, and then a touch of jaundice, all in the space of a few weeks. It seemed I really was run down and needed to have a holiday and a change of air, so here I am in La Paz enjoying life in a most un-missionary fashion. Mr. and Mrs. Warder, with whom I am staying, have invited me several times and I am at last taking advantage of their kind invitation. The Warders are spoiling me completely and I am living in the lap of luxury and having a real rest. This is a lovely house and it has a really English garden with daffodils, polyanthus, roses and even honeysuckle. It could be in England but for the view of snow-capped mountains.

The train from Tupiza plods monotonously across the Altiplano all day and, just as it seems it will never come to an end, a snow-capped range comes into view and creeps nearer and nearer. This is the La Paz range and the highest mountain, Illimani, stands guard over the city. The train crawls into 'El Alto' station and suddenly the whole city of La Paz is seen spread out in a natural basin 1,500 feet below, and the beauty of it, as I saw it, took my breath away. The train then has to zigzag down the mountain side and all the passengers move from one side of the train to the other to admire the view as it winds slowly down. The motor road can also be seen at intervals twisting round among the thousands of Eucalyptus trees which have been planted as a precaution against landslides. These trees add to the beauty of the scenery, which is almost impossible to describe in its loveliness. Can you picture mountains, some capped with snow (the highest ski-run in the world is here), and sloping down to a tree-lined hollow with little Indian huts on the lower slopes? These merge into a city of dual carriageways and skyscrapers. I think this is the loveliest city I have ever seen and it seems a miracle that it should be in such an inaccessible place amongst mountains when it is, itself, on the roof of the world at 12,000 feet.

The main part of the town has wide roads with gardens down the center, fountains, floodlighting and first class hotels, and there are many beautiful plazas. The main plaza is in front of the President's palace. Practically all the side streets are very steep hills and are very uncomfortable to walk in. I noticed this morning that a soldier on guard duty had a little wooden platform to level him up! The streets are full of flashy American cars; many of the people who live here are millionaires and their houses are fabulously extravagant. I don't think I have seen anything to approach them at home, apart from the 'stately homes of England,' and there is a dignity about them that could never be achieved elsewhere. Just to drive round these areas of La Paz is an education in itself. As you get towards the outskirts of the city the opulence fades, giving place to poverty; the Indian sections are little different from the rest of Bolivia. Here again are the colourful 'Chola' clothes and the markets selling all manner of things unfamiliar to me. I went one day to the Contraband Market where you can buy smuggled goods and the law turns a blind eye. Here you can buy nylons, twin sets, tinned foods, shoes, soap etc. quite cheaply.

La Paz by no means lives up to its name—Peace! As I first arrived Mrs. Warder met me at the station with the news that there had been quite a bit of shooting so that it was best to avoid the centre of the city. On several occasions I have heard shooting in the night and it is a bit scary to meet armed soldiers in the streets. We heard there was danger of a revolution and now there is a threatened rail strike. We had quite a fright driving through the city a day or two ago. It was a public holiday and there was a procession of schoolchildren marching past. Suddenly a fast succession of shots rang out and it took us several moments to realise it was fireworks, not a machine gun! I also had another experience of an earth tremor. I was just looking out of my bedroom window when I realised that the flagpole in the garden was swaying backwards and forwards and so was the house! It was an eerie sensation but didn't last long.

On two occasions Mrs. Warder (hereafter I'll refer to her as Dorothy) has taken me up to the airport to wave off some of her friends. It is up at El Alto and is the highest airport in the world, at 13,380 feet. The planes sweep in between the mountains, and it seems funny to us, who are accustomed to the altitude, to see the pilot and co-pilot in their oxygen masks looking for all the world like space men. The passengers stagger out of the pressurised cabin, some of them looking really green in the rarefied atmosphere, and some even collapse and have to be given oxygen. I think I did the best thing coming by train as the slow progress up the mountains gives time to adjust to the increasing altitude. Even on the train some people are very sick. On one occasion, as we drove to the airport, we realised that something must be happening as so many large posh cars passed us in a great hurry. There were crowds at the airport and the V.I.P. was D. Victor Paz Estensorro, the ex-President, now Ambassador to Britain, just setting off for London. It made me feel a little closer to home somehow. I managed to get a close-up photo as he came over to speak to someone who was standing beside me, though I wasn't too comfortable to be so near to him as I was a little afraid someone might choose that moment to shoot him, but all was peaceful and quiet! As he boarded the plane the crowd got wildly excited and gave the Party sign—our Victory V.

I forgot to mention Pennie, and that is a serious omission, for she and I are great friends. She is the Warder's three-year-old daughter, a sweet little scrap with ginger hair and freckles and big blue eyes and I am very fond of her. To my chagrin she speaks Spanish a lot better than I do! It makes no difference to her whether she is speaking Spanish or English; she doesn't mix them and can switch from one to the other with no trouble at all. We have some grand times together and I love to take her out. She comes out with some home truths sometimes, and left me speechless the other morning at breakfast, quoting my own words by saying to me, "Your hair looks terrible!"

Yesterday we all went to the Sunday School outing at a lovely place outside the city. I joined the young people in some games and even won a race—not too bad for this altitude and my 29 years, but I am ever so stiff today!

Last Thursday we had a wonderful time with some friends here. We joined the Landers (senior missionaries) and the Kenneys from U.S.A.; on their way back from furlough, Gordon Bisset of New Zealand visiting here from Sucre, and the Warboys who are Christian folk of the Railway Company here, like the Warders. We enjoyed ourselves so much just chatting in the garden in the afternoon and then, in the evening, listening to hymns on records. How wonderfully soothing some hymns are! 'Tenderly He watches over you,' 'It is no secret what God can do,' 'We shall see His lovely face,' etc. It was just what I needed and so wonderful to realise that the same Lord is with us here. We were strangers in a strange land and yet the Lord has brought each one of us here for a purpose. That evening healed me in a way which is too deep to explain. The Lord is so wonderful to me and I am grateful for this time of renewal in body, mind and spirit.

A rail strike supported by other forms of transport then interrupted everything for several weeks so that I and other missionaries were stranded in La Paz till it was over.

MORE EXCITEMENT IN LA PAZ!

La Paz truly is an enchanting city! You will understand how I feel when I tell you that I have just got engaged to the most wonderful man in the world. How's that for an adventure?! It really is amazing how the Lord uses even unfortunate circumstances to bring about His purposes. I would not have dreamed of coming to La Paz if I had not been ill, but I am sure the Lord meant it this way. Just after, Gordon Bisset came here and we met. Because of the rail strike we had to stay much longer than we expected. Gordon came for a few days but now he has been here for three weeks and the strike is still on. You will think we got engaged awfully quickly—we did! It was in just two weeks but we are both absolutely sure it is the Lord's will for us and that He had it all planned. We are very much in love and both pretty ancient (Gordon five years older than I am) so there seemed no point in waiting. We got engaged one afternoon and then went to a meal with Mr. and Mrs. Lander. The Kenneys were there too. Gordon announced our engagement at the supper table and the result was devastating. They clapped and cheered and bounced in their chairs and eventually told us quite seriously that they had been praying it would happen ever since they first saw us together. It was a great joy to us to feel that our fellow-workers were so happy about it and so sure it was right.

Now I expect you will want to know what kind of man Gordon is. Well, of course, he is smashing! First and foremost he is a man of God and we have had some wonderful times of fellowship together. We made it a principle to spend some time in Bible reading and prayer together before we went out anywhere and it was in those times that we really got to know each other. He certainly has a more intimate knowledge of the Lord and His Word than I have and we look forward to going on together. The Warders kindly lent us their chauffer-driven car, and little Pennie as chaperone, so we took her to the Zoo and all over the place.

Gordon is tall and fair and is very kind. At first I wasn't sure how I felt about him and really it was Mr. Warder who first opened my eyes by saying, "You know he is **very** kind." "Yes, he is," I thought. Dorothy said one day, "Gordon is an absolute gentleman." "Good, that's true" thought I. Another remark from Dorothy, "That fellow is an absolute clown!" "Well, yes, he's that too." He has a tremendous sense of humour and, in fact, life with Gordon promises to be hilarious. I can imagine what fun it will be as we set up home together. I shall make heaps of mistakes as I am by no means an experienced housekeeper and in Bolivia it will be so much harder than in England. The wedding is planned tentatively for November in Cochabamba as we hope to have a Worker's Conference there at that time.

I have already mentioned that Gordon is a New Zealander but he was born in Burma. That foxes officials here and he is down in the archives as having been born in 'Rangoon, Burma, New Zealand!' He has a degree in Botany so it seems I am destined to become 'Betty Bisset the Botanist's wife!' Anyway, I have no doubt we shall be a very 'Happy Family.'

I must tell you of a giggle we had together. We went to have an engagement photo taken. Photography is a very solemn affair here so, when I posed with a very happy smile, the photographer said to Gordon, "Please tell the lady to shut the mouth!" Well, we both just about collapsed!

Life has changed for both of us. To be single here constitutes a real problem for missionaries, especially at our age. An unmarried person of thirty is considered to be either immature or to have a secret sex life somewhere and that is no help to a missionary. Our service for the Lord together should amount to considerably more than either of us could attempt alone. To have a home of our own will be wonderful too. I have stayed with some lovely families and they have been wonderfully kind but it is not a really satisfactory arrangement to share the family life of others, kind though they are. The Lord has been so good to us and the future holds bright prospects of ups and downs together with the Lord. This is a particularly bright patch but we have every confidence in the Lord for the dark days too.

Curriculum Vitae Gordon

"IN THE BEGINNING..."

"If you are not willing, are you willing to be made willing?"

When I was a child in New Zealand, my parents, recently saved, opened their home to missionaries on furlough from all over the world. We had a room for them upstairs, "The Prophet's Chamber." In my little mind was born the idea that I would be a missionary when I grew up. That noble idea died of fright at secondary school. How could the rabbit-timid Bisset be a missionary? Once I had to speak to the class about, "What I want to be when I am grown up." Courage failed; I lamely said that I wanted to be an explorer. Have you ever been laughed at? I felt utterly miserable. But at a Crusader camp my heart was gripped by a chorus...

"O Jesus Lord and Saviour, I give myself to Thee,
For Thou in Thine atonement didst give Thyself for me.
I'll own no other master; my heart shall be Thy throne,
Myself I give henceforth to live, O Christ for Thee alone."

I made that my prayer, and the amazing thing is that the Lord accepted it. I was repeatedly challenged at missionary meetings, especially in Auckland, while at university. My assembly there was alive with missionary interest. There was a missionary Sunday once a month, and we young men sometimes had to prepare a talk on one of the mission fields, if no visiting missionary was available. But my heart became divided: should I press on towards a Botany career in Plant Diseases, and marry one of the attractive girls in the Y.P. Group or keep my eye on the mission field? "...a double minded man, unstable in all he does." (James 1:8, NIV) To my shame, I was that. Missionaries from Bolivia told of the hardship and persecutions endured on the "Altiplano," the high desolate plateau of western Bolivia. My mind recoiled: "No, not there, Lord!" But you cannot call Him Lord, and say, "No."

A weekend Missionary Camp; the speaker was challenging us with the possibility of missionary service, and he said, "If you are not willing, are you willing to be made willing?" It was an arrow from the Lord that hit my heart! I went upstairs to the men's dorm' while chorus singing continued below, and prayed. From that moment my whole outlook changed.

The elders of the church were cautious. They advised me to test my call by serving for a while on the "Gospel Van" of Palmerston North (Central North Island). The "School of hard knocks!" My first companion on that ancient vehicle was an ex-coalminer, a Jordie from Britain. He despised university education, but he was a gifted personal worker. I wasn't. The next was a brash young man, very capable, full of self confidence. I never had that! We worked in the country for miles around, and I learned a lot about door to door visiting and helping the country assemblies. The Lord was good to us and my companions were most patient with me.

My assembly then commended me to the Lord's work in Bolivia and in October 1953 I set sail from Wellington. A little group of friends waved me off as the old S.S. Rangitiki (no air conditioning!) sailed out into a dense fog. There was no young lady in that farewell group, but the Lord had chosen one for me away across the world...but that comes into the story!

—Gordon L. Bisset

7
Wedding in Cochabamba!

OCTOBER 23, 1958

It is just one year since I arrived in Bolivia and I am writing this letter in the train, travelling over the same line which struck terror into me then, the line to Potosí; but today I am going further than Potosí, on to Sucre. I am on my way to get married!

The Lord willing I hope to be married to Gordon Bisset of New Zealand, on November 15th in Cochabamba. Gordon has been out here for 5 years and is at present working in Sucre, and I am on my way there now. In a few days time we go on to Cochabamba, (separately!) as we both have to be 'resident' there for at least eight days before the wedding. We hope that several others of our workers will be in Cochabamba for a few days of fellowship, prayer and conference together before 'our' day. We anticipate seeing the Landers, Kenneys, Browns and Haggertys. Miss Stetter (USA) lives there so we shall meet her. Alas, the Warders from La Paz are not able to come to the wedding, a real shame after all they did for us. It will be as English a wedding as possible although the Registrar will have to do the legal part in Spanish and I shall have to say, "Sí" instead of "I will."

It has been simply amazing to see the way in which the Lord has led us together. It was all most certainly planned by Him alone, and it is with this confidence that we begin our married life.

I am intensely happy and Bolivia is transformed. Gordon is absolutely wonderful and the strange thing is that he thinks I am! I shall look forward to introducing him to you all. So much for the girl who thought she was sacrificing everything for the Lord, marriage included! With regard to the future, we shall most certainly need much prayer as we shall be starting under real difficulties.

The Lord has led us to accept Dr. and Mrs. Brown's offer of their house in Alcatuyo, to work among the people there, as they have now moved down (in altitude) to Sucre for health reasons. Strange how, after just a year, I seem to be retracing my steps. I spent my first five weeks in Alcatuyo and, at the time, it seemed a foolish plan, but no doubt the Lord had the future in mind. Alcatuyo is an entirely Quechua speaking area, so our first task will be to learn the language as quickly as possible. We shall hope to begin meetings using Quechua records from 'Gospel Recordings Inc.' and we can sing (or can we?) from the small Quechua hymnbook. I hope to do some simple medical work. Gordon has already made friends with the Director of the School there as, a few weeks ago, he was stranded in Alcatuyo and spent the night in the school, where he had an excellent opportunity to explain the Gospel to some of the teachers. Work among the children can be in Spanish until we know Quechua as they are taught in Spanish at school.

Housekeeping will be such fun! There is, of course, no electricity, and cooking will have to be on Primus stoves. There is a somewhat temperamental hand pump in the kitchen for water, so that will be a great help. The roof leaks and the rainy season is coming up. During the rainy season we shall be almost completely cut off from civilisation. Potosí is our nearest town and it is about 2½ to 3 hours drive away over perilous roads. We shall hope to get there every three weeks or so to collect mail, post out, and buy stores.

We are very thrilled at the way the Lord has provided this home for us and given us a work to do. Dr. and Mrs. Hamilton will soon be back to their work in Potosí itself, but the area around is vast and no-one is working there at all, either of our own folk or the various missionary societies. Please pray for us as we begin this immense task. We feel so totally inadequate to follow in the wake of Dr. and Mrs. Brown, who speak the language so well and have so much experience and knowledge of the Quechua culture. We feel very new. We don't know how long the Lord will leave us there—there are other open doors, but we feel it is His will for the moment, and we hope to make the most of the opportunity.

Tupiza is now a past chapter of my life. I have loved the work there and been very happy. I was given a grand send off by the women and girls and it was hard to tear myself away. I loved the girls' class I had on Thursday evenings, in spite of the fact that they drove me completely to distraction and left me exhausted each week. How those girlies need your prayers. There are about 20 of them ranging in age from 6 to 15 years. Some are Christians and some not; they have temptations we know nothing about, and at school are much persecuted as 'Evangelistas.' Mrs. Randall will be carrying on with the class, an extra burden for her.

The three young men who were baptized recently are ably taking a share in the work now, and we do praise the Lord for this. It means that Mr. Randall can occasionally be away in the country and confidently leave the meetings to them. This is a great blessing as it has been a real need in Tupiza for some time.

23rd NOVEMBER 1958

I really don't know where to begin writing my adventures this time, as I have had so many exciting ones. As mentioned before, after the rail strike Gordon went back to Sucre and I to Tupiza. Apart from two weeks when Gordon came to Tupiza to see me (staying in the hotel next door, for propriety's sake!), we did not see each other again until three weeks before the wedding. I did receive some hilarious letters and some lovely poems (just for me), and there was a collection of photographs labelled 'Hims Ancient and Modern!' These last helped me to catch up with Gordon's background.

I had mixed feelings as I prepared to leave Tupiza. I had been very happy there and the excitement of getting married was tinged with the sadness of saying 'goodbye' to many friends. At the women's meeting the evening before I left, I was surprised to find that, all unknown to me, a special tea had been arranged so I was sent off in style. I had to parade in my wedding dress, which I had made myself, so that they could all see how I would look on the great day. Quite a crowd came to the station to see me off and I was especially touched as one little girl in the queue to say 'Goodbye,' joined the queue a second time, so got in twice!

The first stage of my journey was to Sucre where I stayed with Mr. and Mrs. Turner and got thoroughly teased. Gordon and I spent a week rushing around buying necessary furniture, and it was wonderful to see how the Lord helped us in this very practical matter. We so often found just what we were looking for and cheaper than we expected. We wanted our things to be as pretty as possible and yet, at the same time, in keeping with country life among Indians who have so little of this world's goods. On Monday Gordon travelled the gruelling journey by 'gondola' (bus!) to Cochabamba and I followed by air next day. To travel by air is often the cheapest and best. For instance my journey took 45 minutes and Gordon's took all day! I enjoyed the flight, my first ever, but was glad when I was safely installed in the peace and comfort of the Bolivian Indian Mission HQ, where I was to stay.

Cochabamba is a delightful city and is said to have one of the best climates in the world as it stands at about 7,000 feet, halfway up between the jungle lowlands and the Altiplano. It was certainly lovely. It is quite a big city and most things can be purchased there—at a price—so it is best to stick to window shopping! The Bolivian Indian Mission house is very nice with a pretty patio full of gladioli and hibiscus, an ideal setting for a wedding. The folk there were so kind to us and entered into the excitement of preparations for the wedding, even though they had not met me before and knew Gordon only a little. They teased us mercilessly, counting the days for us. We met lots of people there from various Missions as there was a conference going on at the time.

During the following week our own fellow-workers began to arrive. Excitement was mounting and I was worrying about flowers, music and all the multitude of details. It is not possible to buy bouquets here; you have to go to market early, get what you can and make up your own. Mrs. Lander and Miss Stetter (who lives in Cochabamba) spent hours icing the cake which Mrs. Randall had made in Tupiza (adding a fourth tier too). I declared it was much too pretentious for a missionary but they were determined that we should have as lovely a wedding as they could make it. The cake was cream coloured and decorated in an elaborate pattern with cream and mauve roses, and the fourth tier was topped with a satin bow. It was really beautiful, far too nice to eat. The two little bridesmaids, Gwennie (of a family on the boat with me) and Ruthie Brown, both aged six, had short, two-tiered dresses of pale mauve nylon trimmed with velvet, and with baskets of pink and mauve flowers they looked really Victorian and sweet. All my things had been sent from home by my parents. Mrs. Mavis Randall was in England and brought a whole trunk full of things when she returned (by sea) to Villazón, so I was very fortunate indeed. My dress was of cream satin with a layer each of yellow net, and then white, over the circular skirt. It was trimmed with pearls. A friend lent a pearl tiara and my mother sent me the lovely Brussels lace veil which she wore for her own wedding, and I carried cream and pink roses. Gordon had a cream rose in his buttonhole.

~~~~~~~~~~~~~~~~~~~~~~
~~~~~~~~~~~~~~~~~~~~~~

Eventually the great day dawned. Dell Brown had several helpers decorating the large lounge under her direction, Mr. Lander was busy setting up the tape recorder, and telegrams were arriving thick and fast. Gordon and I went together to the market in search of flowers; the quest for roses seemed impossible but one market woman, to whom we had spoken the day before, had managed to find just enough for us. Jessie Lander showed me how to wire the flowers and I spent the rest of the morning making my bouquet and the children's baskets. Time flew!

The wedding itself was lovely. I think we appreciated it more listening to the tape-recording afterwards when we were more relaxed. Mr. Lander was my 'father' for the day and gave me away. We had a recording of the Wedding March as we started our procession from my bedroom door across the patio. The Best Man (apart from Gordon) was Don Gale of Australia (BIM), and there were about 50 guests. We were a pretty cosmopolitan wedding party with folk from Australia, New Zealand, Scotland, America, Canada, England and Bolivia. We were thrilled at the way the Bolivian Registrar conducted the official ceremony (in Spanish of course). Usually they produce an unintelligible gabble and call it done, but this man was very dignified and went out of his way to do it well. He spoke beautifully and, after the official bit, he added a little talk of his own which was very nice indeed. Then he congratulated us in true Bolivian style with an abrazo (embrace) and called me 'Señora' for the very first time! At this point we changed to English and, after a hymn, Dr. Brown gave an unusual and excellent address using the life of Abraham and Sarah to illustrate his points.

We had the reception in the patio outside. The speeches were great fun and poor Don got terribly mixed up trying to read out the telegrams in both Spanish and English! He must be forgetting the English I think. Gordon is like that. In an English meeting he came out with, "El número diez, ¿podemos cantar?" (May we sing number ten?) much to everyone's amusement. It was lovely that

Mr. Lander had a letter to read from my parents. It made me feel more as though they were there. I had to make a speech too, which was quite unorthodox and unexpected, but it will be good for my parents to hear when we send them the tape.

While all this was going on my mother and father were having a 'reception' at home. Gordon's mother and sister were there and a number of my friends, and they had a wedding cake and our photographs. We had sent them a tape of our voices too, in greeting.

Oh, the confetti! It was everywhere, even inside my dress. We had a real battle to get to the car, the poshest taxi in town. It was brilliant blue, with flowers on the bonnet and boot, confetti inside and out, and five tin cans tied on the back!

The hotel, still in Cochabamba, was just perfect. We decided that since we have only one honeymoon, and only three days for that, we would be really posh and un-missionary. The complete change was just what we needed. The hotel caters especially for the many Americans in Cochabamba. We had our evening meal on a veranda lit with coloured lanterns, and overlooking a floodlit swimming pool. The food was very good and we had all the modern conveniences we have missed for so long.

Our peace that first evening was short-lived…the phone rang in the dining room for Mr. Bisset! We dithered about what to do but an American took the call and we were horrified as he told the most awful whoppers to the effect that we were not there. This evidently aroused suspicion (I think the caller must have heard me giggling in the background) as later the phone rang again. This time Gordon answered, in Spanish, and said that Mr. Bisset had been there the previous week to make enquiries and gone away again. True so far! Anyway, it had the effect of making the caller uncertain, but they did find out our whereabouts eventually. On going to bed we found that our 'friends' had sewn up our night things with small neat stitches and we had to sit down, somewhat scantily clad, to undo them. Gordon lamented that he had not thought of having 'un-sewing' lessons!

The rest of our honeymoon was a busy time. We went to the meeting on Sunday, and then were busy shopping and packing, though we did have time on Monday to have a swim in that lovely pool, only to find that they had changed the water overnight and it was freezing cold! We were worried about the amount of luggage we had accumulated, (much of it wedding presents) but again the Lord worked miracles for us and we and our luggage were flown safely back to Sucre next day.

Again life was hectic with organising and packing. People said,

"You'll never get a truck to take all your stuff to Alcatuyo"

"You'll never get there..."

"The Jeep won't stand it..."

"It's too far for Gordon to drive in one day..."

One American lady said to us, "Well, you two sure are 'believers.' Everyone is telling you that you will never get there but you are still going!" Here again we proved that things that are impossible are just what the Lord can do. He provided a truck for us for the very day we wanted, and the luggage just fitted on to it. There wouldn't have been room for more. No doubt that is why my boxes hadn't arrived from Tupiza as expected. They had been sent straight to Alcatuyo!

We overslept next morning so didn't leave till 8.45 a.m. and after some hours of travelling we caught up with our furniture truck and pressed on ahead. We picnicked in a lovely spot in really hot sunshine and then continued on and on and up and up, arriving in Betanzos in time to have tea with the Burrows family of the Bolivian Indian Mission. We hoped to arrive in Alcatuyo before dark, but shortly after leaving Betanzos we had a puncture and, not having a spare wheel, we had to stop and mend it. It had a business-like little nail stuck straight up into the tyre - and we were out in the wilds. Gordon got the tyre off, patched up the inner tube, and our truck caught us up just at the right time to pump up the tyre and put it back on for us. This was wonderful, as using a hand-pump at 12,000 feet is no joke for those not born and bred at this altitude. We got to Alcatuyo at 9:30 p.m. and the truck arrived a bit later. Gordon and the men unloaded all the stuff by the light of two candles and a torch while I got the supper for everyone on a Primus. We finished at midnight, tired but happy, and crawled on to our mattress on the floor.

SUNDAY IN ALCATUYO

We are in the midst of chaos but have delightful visions of what our house is going to be. I think we are both feeling the altitude with all this physical work to do, but it hasn't worried either of us before so I expect we shall soon settle down to it. My luggage from Tupiza arrived this morning, a real blessing as we need so many things out of it.

We had our first meeting this morning. Not many came, but we had one man, two women and three children! We couldn't get the loudspeaker working in time to use it, so the people were probably not expecting anything, and not many know we are here yet. These folk have no clocks, they go by the sun, so Mrs. Brown used to sing hymns over the loudspeaker at meeting time and we hope to do the same. We played some Quechua records to our congregation, sang some hymns and read Psalm 23 over twice. Gordon can read Quechua quite well, even without understanding it, though he can speak a little. This is the sort of thing..." Ciertomanta c'acha cajlla qhuyacuywan khatiwankancu causayniypa tucuy p'unchaycunasninpi.' ('Surely goodness and mercy shall follow me all the days of my life') We would value prayer about this language problem! Beginning tomorrow I have a Quechua Indian girl coming to help me in the kitchen, and I shall have to learn the language soon or anything might happen! Her name is Fortunata and I just hope she proves to be 'fortunate' for us.

I would like to put on record how wonderful the Lord is and how very grateful we are to Him for putting us here and for giving us the opportunity of working for Him in a vast area of around 100,000 scattered Indian people.

LATE NEWS...

On Sunday, December 14th, we went into Puna. It was a Fiesta day and they were parading the local 'Saint' round the Plaza. The police were very friendly and cleared a way for us. We fixed up the loudspeaker and had an open air meeting. An enormous crowd gathered to see these new foreigners, ('gringos' they call us) and when we gave out tracts afterwards we were pretty well mobbed. We hadn't taken nearly enough, even though we gave them out only to those who could read.

8
Indian Adventures

JANUARY 1959

Gordon and I are having the most trying time I think we have ever experienced. It all began two days ago. I was just putting the finishing touches to our lunch when Gordon came in and said that an Indian had arrived and was obviously very upset because a child of his had injured his leg. We talked to him for a while and it sounded really serious so we agreed to go with him to the house. Unfortunately the Jeep was partially dismantled, so we had to walk. It was a baking hot afternoon and we plodded uphill and down, walking fast behind the sure-footed Indian and hungrily remembering the lunch we had left untouched. I was worn out in ten minutes (remember the altitude of 12,000 feet) but we kept walking for an hour. The Indian had said that he lived by the school, a few minutes from home, but he evidently meant a school in a different village. We followed him, completely lost ourselves, until we eventually arrived at a little adobe house.

There was a hush over the house as we arrived and all the family began to weep. We went in and, for a moment, could not see anything in the dark. Gradually forms began to take shape and we saw a boy of about 12 lying on the floor with relatives sitting around him. I wished I had brought morphia but I hadn't, so made do with a couple of pain-killers before doing anything, as he was obviously in great pain. I began to undo the filthy bit of cloth which was tied round his leg, and came upon several pages torn out of his school exercise books wrapped round the wound. It was a work of art to unstick the paper and the wound was horrible. Apparently a boulder had fallen from a wall as he went to climb over and had taken a chunk of flesh from the inner part of his knee and lower leg. The wound was about eight inches long, very wide, and the bone was showing, though mercifully, not broken. I did all I could, which wasn't really very much. I cleaned it all up and dressed it with lots of gauze, soaked in antiseptic, cotton wool, and a crepe bandage, and then improvised a splint. We said we were going to Potosí the next day and would take him to the hospital there; under anaesthetic they could do more for him than I could, but it really was a case for plastic surgery which they would not attempt there. I was afraid he might have an infection or other complications too.

Next day the father arrived early at our house and we set out in the patched up Jeep. We had made the back as comfortable as we could for the boy and had improvised a stretcher to get him from the house to the road. We were dead tired as the previous day's walk had been about 8 miles in all, no joke at this altitude; as Gordon commented, "A nice little stroll before lunch!" About five minutes from home the Jeep broke down again. The fan belt had broken and disappeared! With electric cable as a substitute we limped as far as we could, and then I accompanied the Indian on my own while Gordon stayed to think about what to do for the Jeep. The house is far from the road and I was gone about an hour and a half. I gave the boy a shot of morphia and said we would return for him if we could fix the Jeep. The Indian had given me a plaited leather lasso and I got back to Gordon who was just beginning to worry about me. He managed to improvise a fan belt with the lasso, but it took some time, and for the second day lunch became a forlorn hope.

All set, we hoped to reach Potosí and Gordon went back for the boy. He found that the father had gone out (to get a witch doctor we fear) and the relatives wouldn't let the boy go without the father. After waiting an hour Gordon gave up, as there was little prospect of the father returning for a long time, and returned to the car where I had been waiting for two hours wondering wherever he had got to. We decided to try and get to Potosí, buy a new fan belt and return for the boy the next day.

Our trip was adventurous! Because the improvised fan belt kept slipping we had to stop several times to let the engine cool and to patch up other bits. We were desperately tired and hungry, and very, very hot. About an hour before we reached Potosí, a hailstorm began; hail two inches deep covered the road and we were frozen! We were relieved to reach Potosí just before the shops shut. We were on the road for nine hours (to travel a little over 30 miles) and every minute was a worry. This morning Gordon has fitted the new fan belt, mended a puncture and set out on his own to fetch the boy. I hope he will be back tonight. The problem is gasoline, as we cannot buy it today, and we are not sure if there is enough in the tank. To my horror I have just discovered that he has gone without the extra tin of 10 litres he was depending on, so I am terribly afraid he will get stuck on the way back and have to spend the night on the road. There won't be any passing trucks to help him today as it is a public holiday. It was dreadful saying, "Good-bye" to him as there is quite an element of danger in the trip. I wish I could have gone, but we decided I had better stay and have a rest.

Next day...

The Lord looked after Gordon wonderfully yesterday. He met a Christian medical student from Sucre University, home for the holidays. His father was able to supply some gas and Ricardo, the student, went with Gordon. Ricardo speaks Quechua fluently (it is probably his first language) and he was able to add his persuasions and medical knowledge in a further attempt to get the boy to hospital, but the parents would not agree. They had taken off my dressings and replaced them with a paste of sheep droppings, and leaves. We had to wash our hands of the whole thing but, if it all goes septic, they will probably come back to me again, when it is too late to save the leg. Poor lad! Ricardo gave the family 'what for' in Quechua!

From Alcatuyo
a week later...

Some folk came yesterday asking us to take the injured boy to Puna but we refused as there is no one in Puna who could do anything for him. We said again that he should go to the hospital in Potosí and we reminded them that we had gone to all lengths to help them to do that. We then advised them to go to Ricardo as he could talk to them easily and his home is only a few miles away. Being a nearly qualified doctor, we knew that he would give them the same advice as we had given. Ricardo's father has a truck so perhaps they will be able to take the boy to hospital. They say he is very bad. We have been realising that this is a very apt illustration of the attitude people have towards the Lord. He did so much for them, went out of His way, spent thirty years on earth especially for them, suffered, even died, because He knew their plight, and yet they take not a bit of notice of what He says. They don't accept His help or thank Him for His trouble. They prefer to find their own way out of the difficulty but the means in which they trust are futile.

~~~~~~~~~~~~~~~~~~~~

FEBRUARY 1959

Hey ho, the things that happen! Take today for instance...day of small things. It is Saturday and Gordon was up with the lark as usual (though I don't think there are any here), while I struggled to consciousness, and we eventually got about the day's work. My first job, believe it or not, was to make a cushion. We had bought some cheap but pretty material in Potosí and, having made curtains and a box cover for our bedroom, I made a cushion cover
~~~~~~~~~~~~~~~~~~~~

with the last piece of material. Of course we hadn't any feathers or other suitable stuffing so we filled it with wood shavings. It looks fine! I think, though, that I shall have to attach a label to it saying, "Please do not lean on this cushion!" After that I had a good time cooking and, for once, the oven behaved well. We often have quite a bonfire with the cooker; gasoline pressure stoves are temperamental things!

This afternoon Gordon was making the umpteenth unsuccessful attempt to repair a leak in the second gasoline tank of the Jeep. We have been losing gas steadily. The obvious thing is to disconnect the second tank and use only one...but how? It was certainly not made to be disconnected. Eventually I crawled under the Jeep too and together we surveyed the hopeless prospect. We managed to disconnect the tube joining the two tanks and plugged the open end with a kaolin poultice! Tomorrow's trip to Puna will soon test our mechanics.

Next I cut Gordon's hair. I think he is pretty brave to let me risk the clippers, but the slightly moth-eaten effect is an improvement on the 'shaggy dog story' he was developing into.

At supper time I found a Valentine card on my plate, Gordon's own effort (even the poem) which he had produced with great secrecy while I was in the bath! Yes, I do have a bath, though only once a week. We have a big round galvanised iron tub into which I can just squeeze myself. It is not exactly civilised, but it is good. It is an awful chore pumping the water and heating it up on the stove and then bailing it all out again afterwards. I had complained miserably that I kept losing the soap (I cannot reach the floor over the side once I am squeezed in) so Gordon made me a lovely soap tray to hang on the side. He has become quite an expert maker of gadgets. It is made from a big Paua shell from New Zealand and the natural holes are in exactly the right place to drain the water off the soap. Not many people have the luxury of a soap tray lined with exquisite Mother-of-Pearl.

Having started with today, I shall have to work backwards. Dr. and Mrs. Hamilton are now back from furlough and are visiting Pacasi. We went to see them there last Tuesday. First Gordon had to mend a puncture and we had no patches left. We had almost given up hope of going when I remembered that I had some 'Sewing Eliminator' (the kind of material you can just iron on over a tear). We got it out and looked at it dubiously. Fortunata (our Indian helper) was ironing with the gasoline pressure iron; there could be no harm in trying. We brought the inner tube to the kitchen, cut out a neat square of the material and ironed it carefully in place. It looked fine and lasted our journey out although the tyre was flat again next morning.

It took us a long time to get to Pacasi though it is only 15 miles away. As we passed the Agricultural School in Puna, a young Indian hailed us and asked us to take him and his bedding into town. We agreed and then had to wait for ages while he got himself organised. About 5 miles further on we slid gently to a standstill having run out of gas! This meant struggling to unearth the gasoline tin from beneath our passenger's bed. After a couple of stops in Puna and a refill of gas we arrived at last.

We were hoping that lunch would be ready for us when we arrived, but we found that we were all invited to one of the Indians' homes. Oh, woe! It was a long trudge up hill and down dale and we eventually arrived feeling very hungry, but it was at least another hour before the meal was served. We started with a very hot (in both senses) soup with all manner of things floating in it; this was followed by a sticky gluey mess. I can't imagine what it was. There was a pile of cooked but unpeeled vegetables on the floor. After these we had horrible Indian bread (made of peanut flour) and tea. The final course was a kind of blackberry coloured porridge. Later we had a brown drink made from peanuts and about 25 of us all shared two glasses! The only food I enjoyed was the soup.

After a meeting in which we sang and listened to two talks in Quechua, we were looking forward to heading for home, but it had been pouring heavily with rain and the river was now too high to cross. We all waited a long time and then decided to risk it and try to get home. At the first river, a little one, Gordon and an Indian man waded in and helped the rest of us to balance as we crossed on the rocks. The next river was a different proposition; it was wide and knee deep, with a strong current. I was game to wade over but it wasn't considered the thing for a lady to do, so an Indian carried me over pick-a-back (much less ladylike I would have thought!). I was sorry it was not Gordon who carried me over, but I realised that the Indians are very sure footed and used to this sort of thing. Mrs. Hamilton, being an older lady, was horrified at the prospect of being carried by an Indian, so she was chaired across the river between two of them. It was very late when we got home.

A week later…

We are in Potosí now. The Jeep misbehaved as usual and we had to push it from home to the main road. The main road is only dirt, mind you, even though it is a part of the Pan American Highway! At last we got it going by coasting down hill (in the wrong direction) and off we went over the very bumpy road. Fortunata was with us. We planned to buy gasoline in Cuchu Ingenio but there wasn't any. We had about half a gallon left to do 25 miles. We pressed on and came upon a truck parked by the road so stopped to ask what was wrong. Could we lend them some gas? Imagine! Sorry! About half a mile further on the Jeep stopped too. After a while we remembered that we had a little household gas (most kerosene (paraffin) pressure equipment runs fairly safely on gas at this altitude!) so we put that in the tank. The two cupfuls took us a surprising distance.

We busied ourselves with a tin of sardines we had brought and some pikelets, and then had a happy time playing boats with the sardine tin! Just how childish can missionaries get?! After a time a truck came by and let us have about a gallon of gas and, while it was being transferred, I gave Gospel tracts to all the people riding on the back of the truck. Alas, we stopped again just a few miles outside the city, but we did eventually arrive. Gordon took the Jeep to the garage for repair the next day and the mechanic said, "What did you come on, the smell of the gasoline?" There wasn't a drop left.

In all our adventures it is wonderful how the Lord cares for us. He answers prayer and sees us through, though the way isn't easy. I firmly believe in a personal devil and I am sure it is he who puts difficulties in our way. We pray, and the Lord is far stronger, so we get through in the end, even if we do get a bit battered by the way. We don't expect it to be easy and it is a battle but 'we are more than conquerors through Him...'

Footnote: Just a reminder to the readers that these rather lengthy *Adventure Reports* are semi-private letters which the writer had sent home for distribution among her many friends and relatives to tell them about the country and her life in Bolivia, and were therefore not specifically intended to be *Prayer Letters.*

9
With the Jeep and without it!

APRIL 1959

Two Sundays ago Gordon and I, with Fortunata (our indispensable servant girl) and Seforina (a Christian Quechua woman) set out in the Jeep for Puna. It was a wet day and we were not very keen to go, but we had promised to visit a lady who wanted to be baptised. The famous Jeep had just been repaired so, apart from the fact that it wouldn't start, we were fairly confident. Soon after setting out an ominous rat-tat-tat began in the motor, but we had to press on so we optimistically put it down to the loose fan. We came to the wide river bed which was in a bad state because of the rain, but crossed it without mishap. Just the other side an agonised squawk came from the motor and we stopped dead. Mercifully, we were not going very fast. We looked at each other and realised that we were just six miles from home and almost two miles from Puna, on a road where traffic is almost nil apart from ourselves. Seforina walked on into Puna to tell the folk we couldn't get there; Fortunata stayed by the Jeep; Gordon and I set out for the Agricultural School for help. No one in authority was there to help so we carried on into Puna and there found the director of the school. He promised to send out a tractor to tow us in, but just then we met a man with a 'Dept. of Agriculture' Jeep and he offered to come himself. A crowd of us piled into his Jeep (I was the only girl with about eight men!) and off we went to the scene of the tragedy. I was glad to return by car across the river we had just waded through.

There was some delay as we had to go first to haul a large truck out of the river a bit further down, but then they, too, came to see how we fared. Our little Jeep was towed jerkily to the Agricultural School and there we had to abandon it. The driver then insisted that, after lunch, he would take us home, making a special journey to do so. Neither of these would take any money (a real mercy as neither of us had thought to take any!) and this was because of kindnesses other missionaries had done for them before we came. We were tremendously grateful for their help; the prospect of the long trek home had not added to our cheer.

What to do then became a real problem. There we were, stuck out in the wilds with the car immobile in Puna. On Tuesday we set out for Potosí, asking a lift from a passing truck. We had to pile on top of the goods with a dozen or so other people. It is certainly a good way to see the country, but it is not exactly comfortable. The first hold-up was at a hairpin bend with a sheer drop on one side. A truck had broken down there, and another, trying to pass it, had broken the bank and sunk in the mud, with the gear stuck in neutral. The combined manpower of the three truckloads managed to push the second one away; they then built up the bank and our truck crawled safely past. The other two had been there all night. Apart from having to stop and clean the spark plugs at intervals, we got to Potosí without further delay.

The mechanic who had repaired (?) our Jeep was very sorry to hear of our misfortune, and we managed to arrange with him that a large truck would go out to fetch the Jeep and bring it in pick-a-back. Happy days! Just when we were all set for this to happen, a strike began and no cars were allowed on the streets. We were truly stuck then as we could not get out of Potosí. We were sleeping in the room behind the meeting hall, a fairly comfortable place for a short time, and having meals with Dr. and Mrs. Hamilton. It was not until the following Monday that the strike came to an end and then, suddenly, the streets were full of cars. We packed hurriedly, had a quick lunch and set out in search of a truck going our way. We discovered that a gondola (a bus, remember?) was going to Puna, so we eventually decided to go there and walk the seven miles home. It would be exhausting but seemed the only thing to do.

A little boy was shouting the gondola's destination, "Puna Puna Puna" at the top of his voice and as we got on he said, "Oh good, evangelistas!" He was evidently expecting great fun and games on the trip and so were we! Just before the gondola was due to leave another truck appeared and was going through Alcatuyo, so we hopped out of the gondola and ran for the truck. I was sure there wasn't room for another person; it was crammed. Gordon fought his way on and I handed the luggage up to him, then up myself...I'm getting quite expert, one foot on the hub, next on the tyre, on the side and then over the railings. This let me down into the midst of a mass of humanity and others got on after me! We set off at a terrific speed and got home in record time.

Our companions on the truck were mostly Indians of a different type from those of Alcatuyo. They wore light baggy trousers, an extra piece of material round their hips and a wide leather belt. A loose sort of blouse covered the upper half of their bodies, and they wore round felt hats tied under the chin with a cord. Their clothes, especially the sleeves, were heavily embroidered. They come from a slightly hotter part of Bolivia and had obviously been to the city with grapes. We liked them. They seemed friendly and looked rather fine fellows. We counted twenty five heads on the back of that truck and there could have been more underneath! All had quantities of bultos (their possessions tied up in a large cloth) so it really was a bit of a squash. Talking of squash, Gordon, having been sitting precariously on someone's bulto, stood to stretch his legs and a strange expression crossed his face. He had been sitting on someone's bananas, mashing them to a pulp, and the soggy mess had just penetrated his trousers to his skin. When he stood up the cooler draught made the sensation very unpleasant indeed!

~~~~~~~~~~~~~~~~~~

The next Sunday morning was just the nicest it could be—a clear sunny day. We set off early from Alcatuyo, our knapsacks on our backs and walked to Puna. Fortunata led the way over rough paths. The crowds increased as we went along because it was the day of the annual cattle fair. As other paths joined ours, people, donkeys and cattle converged. I found it rather fun to walk 'Indian file' as the paths allowed for only one person at a time. We waded through a river, climbed over walls, and, at last, after two and a half hours walking, we arrived in Puna. What a transformation! Puna was a seething mass of people. The plaza was filled with stalls selling all manner of goods, the cattle sale was going on elsewhere, and, in yet another place, horses and mules were for sale. I loved this section! There is something fine about a South American on a fine mule with an elaborate saddle. They ride as though the world is theirs. Mules are more expensive than horses.

Gordon and I caused quite a stir; for one thing it is unusual to see gringos (foreigners) walking, and for another, gringos never carry anything, they get Indians to do it for them. There we were, having obviously walked quite a distance and carrying enormous packs. I wouldn't like to do it too often though, at this altitude. We found quite a crowd of Christians gathered together from different places and were able to have a meeting with them. After a quick picnic lunch, we all went off together to preach in the plaza; a good crowd listened. We have made so many friends in Puna now among the police, the agricultural college folk and the Servicio Agricola, that we find it a little difficult to remember who is who
~~~~~~~~~~~~~~~~~~

when they accost us in the plaza. The people in this town are very friendly and they seem quite interested in the Gospel.

As the day went on we began to get a little anxious as there was no sign of the truck which was to carry our Jeep to Potosí. We decided to walk to the school so that, at least, we would be there when the truck arrived and would waste no time...waste no time! A few yards down the road we met two men looking for us. They led us round the corner and there was the truck with the Jeep looking very sorry for itself, tied securely on top! We hadn't had to lift a finger to help, and Gordon had been anticipating a really tough time. We were all set to go but had to wait pretty well two hours while the driver went off for a bit of refreshment. My nose is still peeling after all that time in the hot sun!

About five minutes after setting out, we were delayed for half an hour by the truck in front of us. They stopped at a river to fill up with water and we couldn't help laughing because they were using a two gallon tin which was so battered it couldn't have held more than a cupful at the time. Then we stopped laughing as their engine gave out and it was a long time before they, and we, got on our way again. On the way, we picked up a good many passengers; to our horror some of them got inside the Jeep, which, by this time was tilting at a perilous angle! One window was broken. The next morning they took the Jeep round to the mechanic and, when it was unloaded, we held counsel over the works. For all the world it reminded me of the doctor's round at Westminster Hospital where I had trained as a nurse. There was the poor old Jeep with the bonnet up, and peering into its inside were the mechanic, two or three assistants, the truck driver, Gordon and myself. I fear we have had our last trip in it. The damage is repairable but we feel disinclined to trust it anymore.

~~~~~~~~~~~~~~~~~~~~~~~~~~
~~~~~~~~~~~~~~~~~~~~~~~~~~

Our problem now is to find a new car. The Lord knows that we need one and we can trust Him about it—He has never failed us yet. Only this morning, we badly needed some eggs (they are like gold dust at the moment). I prayed for some and within two or three hours we had a dozen and a half. Six would have done, but so often, in little things or big, the Lord sends us "exceedingly abundantly above all we ask or think."

~~~~~~~~~~~~~~~~~~~~~~

The latest miracle the Lord has done for us is truly an item for thankful praise. We prayed much for a new car, and a really hardy one is essential for the work here: We had seen, and fallen for, a Land Rover in Potosí and, since the owner had caught us snooping, we had to confess that one like that was just what we needed. He said he was thinking of selling it, but the price he mentioned was well above what we might hope to offer. Gordon had prayed especially for a Land Rover, but since the price was too high, we set about looking at other second-hand vehicles. In every case there was something wrong, usually in the official papers. For several weeks we were without a car and cut off from much of our work: we felt sure the Lord must have something for us so, again, we went off by truck (Gordon on top of a cargo of gasoline drums) to Potosí. There in the accumulated mail at the Post Office was an unexpected cheque large enough to bring the Land Rover into the realms of possibility. The cheque came from the estate of a lady of whom we had never heard. We went to see the owner of the Land Rover, he brought the price down, and within ten days it was ours! It is such a joy to us. We have had it for a week now, and it is wonderful to have a reliable, comfortable vehicle. We are indeed thankful to the Lord for it. We caused utter consternation in all the offices by insisting on honesty with regard to taxes, but we trust the Lord to use even that small testimony. We were urged to cheat on the grounds that 'everybody does it,' (too true) but the lawyer
~~~~~~~~~~~~~~~~~~~~~~

groaned and said, "They're all the same these evangelicals, they insist on paying!"

APRIL 1959

I wonder whether I shall ever master the intricacies of Quechua. A woman came in five minutes ago and poured out a torrent of Quechua, from which I gathered precisely two words, to the effect that someone's stomach was hurting, and Gordon understood very little more. When we first came here, after Dr. and Mrs. Brown had left, I found that Roger had left me a paper with Quechua words for all the common ailments and symptoms people might tell me about. At the bottom he wrote,

"P.S. Actually, what I do is tie a string round the waist of the patient and, if the trouble is above it I give Aspirin and if it is below I give Epsom Salts!"

This is quite untrue, of course, but it gave us a good laugh. So much for the top student of his year at Westminster Hospital! The language problem does cause some amusing situations, but the important thing is that we have come with the message of LIFE and we long to master their language quickly and tell them about it.

In Alcatuyo itself we have meetings on Friday evening and on Sunday morning. On Friday especially the little hall is full of Indians and we sing and play gramophone records in Quechua from *Gospel Recordings Inc.* Gordon gives a talk which, though brief, has needed painful preparation. Three Quechua ladies who come are Christians and one of them sometimes butts in and tells everybody what she thinks Gordon is trying to say! We long to get among them and visit them in their homes. We can make ourselves understood and probably understand what they say simply to us, but when they talk among themselves, we are lost.

On Fridays at lunchtime a crowd of boys from the school come over to our house (there are only about 5 girls in a school of 200). They play football (usually Gordon against the rest!) and then settle down for a talk. I wish you could have seen them today. About 80 little ragamuffins were all fighting for a front row view of the flannelgraph. We finish up exhausted after the scramble but it is worth it. They also like sheets of newspaper with which to cover their exercise books so, after the meeting, we distribute these, strictly one each, but some crafty lads go out of the gate, round the back of the house, over the wall, and queue up again!

You have heard about the Agricultural School in the Jeep drama. Don't imagine a posh building or anything. They have just a large adobe building, like their homes, with dormitory and classroom. The young fellows there seem really keen for us to come. We went on Wednesday evening and were shown into a long dormitory with rough beds down either side. Some lads were playing cards, others attempting table-tennis, and others just lounging around, but they gathered quietly at one end of the room to watch the film strip and listen to the talk. These boys are carefully chosen from many parts of Bolivia and some of them seemed really interested. If they were converted, who knows how far-reaching the effect might be?

One recent adventure was Gordon's alone and I am very tempted to envy him and wish I had been there. I could have gone but felt I was busy. We were informed by the football team of Alcatuyo School that we had been elected 'padrinos' of the team. This is a great honour but we were not exactly thrilled as it involves paying for the footballs and a jersey for each of the team! In fact, what it amounts to is that they consider you a rich neighbour well able to afford the required garments. We pondered this for a long time and eventually decided to accept the responsibility, bearing in mind that we are only stewards of the money entrusted to us but, at the same time, these boys are our ready made Sunday School. Gordon was asked to go and present these things to the team and this was when I, unfortunately, stayed at home, thinking he would only be gone for a few minutes. When he got there, the whole school was assembled, plus a crowd of adults, about 200 in all, and a special programme was presented in Gordon's honour. They sang and recited unexpectedly well and all bowed to him as they began. Afterwards he had to make a speech in which he took the opportunity to tell them just why we are living in Alcatuyo as missionaries. He then presented the things and came home feeling like Public Benefactor No. 1, and was really rather touched.

10
Always Another Valley

OCTOBER—DECEMBER 1959

A new situation has cropped up sooner than we expected. We had agreed to go to Tupiza for a short time to accompany a new worker, Noel McKernon, who was there alone, but we didn't expect it to happen quite yet. Before we left, Gordon went into Potosí to collect our mail. He was very late in getting home and I was beginning to get worried, wondering what might have happened to him, when I saw the lights of the car turn off the road toward the house. He had had a bad time as there was a drivers' strike in Potosí. He had to leave the car on the outskirts of the city and walk the rest of the way. When he got back up the hill to the car he found that the strikers had let down the two front tyres! He protested somewhat vigorously to the pickets at the barrier and, after some discussion, they agreed to let him leave the city. When they saw him exhausted before the Land Rover tyres were anything like re-inflated, (by hand pump and at an altitude of 14,000 feet there!) they even helped him to finish the job! This really was of the Lord's mercy as I would have been desperately worried if he had not been able to return home till after the strike ended a week later. There would have been no way of letting me know as the telegraph people were on strike too. We packed up our household and set off for Tupiza on Friday, a week ago now.

What a trip that was! We had several problems to contend with as we set out. The strike was still on in Potosí and we were not sure how far it had spread. If we met strikers it was possible they would damage the car; we had little gasoline and did not know if it would be possible to buy any. In fact we had no idea whether we would arrive at all. We set out at 7 a.m. and soon arrived at a village called Hornos. Here there was deep gloom from the owners of a truck 'plantado' because the distributor had been removed from the engine. The driver assured us that there was no gas to be had for considerably further than our little would take us. We therefore went out of our way to Puna (taking the truck driver with us). We didn't risk taking the car into the town lest we should be detained, so I stayed with the car while the men walked the rest of the way. Gasoline could not be bought but a friendly truck driver let us have some from his tank; this was because some missionaries had once been kind to him in the past. We have been amazed at how often people have done kindnesses to us because they had been helped by other missionaries. When we got back to Hornos we had lost two hours.

The first part of the journey went smoothly except that the road led straight along the river bed over bumps and boulders till we felt completely shaken up. It seemed so long before we arrived at our next stop, Vitichi. Here we were welcomed with some curiosity as no cars had been that way for days. The men surrounded us and wanted to know what was happening about the strike. We were able to procure a permit to travel, a necessity for any journey in this country, our 'hoja de ruta' giving details of our route and destination. We also bought a bottle of fizzy pop but no gas!

Soon after leaving Vitichi, we stopped to eat our sandwiches on a hill with a wonderful view. An ominous sizzling from the radiator alerted us that the radiator had sprung a leak and was half empty. We cooled water from the thermos to put into it and Gordon managed to collect a little more from a house some distance back. We had a rest and pressed on, but our concern changed from gasoline to water! Never was there such a desert! On and on we went through dry, cracked and parched country, and just as we were despairing, we came upon a village. Here there must be water! A friendly man led us to the village supply, a hole in the ground about a foot square. It was a well and we were able to collect all the water we needed. At another house there was a drum of gas and we were able to buy sufficient to finish our journey. Gordon had to siphon the gas out, a thing he is definitely not good at. It was a wide tube and Gordon's exclamations (in Quechua) caused much hilarity!

After that the journey seemed to drag terribly, especially after we passed the town of Cotagaita. We went through valley after valley and over the ranges in between. Gordon said, "I'm fed up with this valley." I replied, "So am I. What comes next?" "Another one like it!" and this went on for hours. Darkness descended on us and it became difficult to follow the road which was marked only by a line of stones on either side in the river bed. It was a pitch dark night and I was quite scared. Then fires began to appear in the mountains on either side, and we remembered that it was a fiesta night: St. John's night, when they light fires and jump through the flames.

The road went on and on and then suddenly stopped! We were lost. Fortunately there was a house nearby and the occupants came out at the unexpected sound of a car. Horses are more common here. "Oh no, there isn't a road this way, it turns off further back." Back we went and at last got to the entrance to the town, only to find the chassis of a truck carefully placed to bar the way to traffic. Some people living nearby were very helpful and guided our small Land Rover round the back of a house, and thereby round the obstruction. We lost the road again and fell sideways into a ditch, but eventually drove into Tupiza on the smell of gas just before 10 p.m.

We were desperately tired, but were very conscious of how wonderfully the Lord had helped over every obstacle. We received a great welcome from Noel and, later, from the believers here. Now we are enjoying the lower altitude, and to me it is a great joy to have a market just around the corner, rather than 35 miles away. I am so happy here as a missionary; there just isn't another job like it. Here we are directly responsible to the King of Kings and seeking to make known His Son. It is the biggest privilege and responsibility that I can think of.

~~~~~~~~~~~~~~~~~~~~~~~~~~

HOME AGAIN IN ALCATUYO,

"...praying also for us, that God would open unto us a door of utterance, **to speak...**"
—Colossians 4:3

"...a great door and effectual is opened unto me and there are many adversaries..."
—1 Corinthians 16:9

As the above verses come to my mind, I am very aware of the multitude of opportunities that are open to us here. The problem is that we are still unable to make full use of the opportunities because of our limitations in the Quechua language. We know more than we did, and for Gordon to prepare messages is less of a strain, but oh, how far we have yet to go! I get on famously with our Quechua servant girl, Fortunata, and think I am doing well, and then someone else calls and I understand one word in a torrent. We can usually piece together the story by catching odd words and then asking simple questions based on these, but we do want to get the language fluently. It is much easier to make yourself understood than to understand. For me it is difficult to find time for language study, and in this altitude it is difficult to concentrate. Later when Noel was staying with us here for about ten
~~~~~~~~~~~~~~~~~~~~~~~~~~

days in the higher altitude, he too found this difficult. He said, "I can't concentrate up here, I can't even pray." Too well we know it!

Before I tell you more about the work, I must give you some personal news and items for prayer. First of all, there is someone new to pray for, or nearly so! You will rejoice with us that, if all goes well, the Lord will give us a Baby Bisset as a Christmas present. We plan to go to Cochabamba for this event and now it has become clear that I must go sooner than we at first anticipated. I have been advised by Dr. Hamilton to get out of this altitude as soon as possible and until the newcomer is about a month old. We feel it wise to take this advice and, in fact, I am getting a bit weary and shall be glad to do so. The time in Cochabamba at only 8,000 feet will be a wonderful rest for me, enabling me to catch up on arrears of Bible study, language study, and to make preparation for Baby Bisset. Certainly I shall not need to waste time. Having seen me settled, Gordon will return to work alone here in Alcatuyo until schools close at the end of November. He will have to look after himself entirely and it will be a very lonely life for him. There will be little opportunity for communication between us. Mail and telegrams are usually worse inland than from the outside world.

Our activities follow the same pattern as usual and the schools seem to be the most encouraging field. We still have over a hundred (mostly boys) from Alcatuyo school every Friday, and they listen really well. They are a scruffy little crowd, and I always marvel at how they manage to play football on the stony ground with bare feet, but they are just like children the world over and have the most delightful chuckles! Two of the schoolmasters came over to chat with Gordon yesterday and he had a great time with them. One professes to be a Christian and the other is definitely interested.

At the school in Chilcane there are eighty children and two teachers, brother and sister. The teachers are really interested and teach the children choruses from our gramophone records.

Gordon usually goes there alone as the roads are so appalling. At the Agricultural School near Puna, we get a rousing welcome every week from the thirty older boys who study there. We always enjoy our visits, sitting in the dormitory in the light of a Coleman lamp and speaking of the Gospel to them; something which is quite new to them. I think some of them are wondering when all the Saints are coming into the story. Some of the boys are buying New Testaments or Gospels, and they always sit down on their beds to read them or any tracts we may have given them.

The other day an old Indian came to the house and nearly took our breath away! We would be glad of prayer for him and for his family. He was the first Christian in this neighbourhood, became a fearless Gospel preacher and was much used of the Lord. Several of his family were saved too. Then suddenly he went right back, completely ruined his testimony and became openly hostile to the Gospel and to Dr. and Mrs. Brown. He also prevented his family from coming to meetings. His name, 'Juan de la Cruz', inappropriately means 'John of the Cross,' and is usually abbreviated to 'Juandela.' He would never come near here but suddenly he turned up. He asked Gordon to read some letters to him. A few days later he came again, this time wanting Gordon to fetch a Judge from Potosí to deal with a lawsuit in which he is involved. Of course Gordon said "No" and a few other things, and was most relieved when the old man said, "That is what Dr. Brown said." Juandela did say that he wants to come back to the Lord. He is an old rogue and we do not know his motives, but this is the first evidence of a change of heart. We pray it may be for real. The 'ground' here is hard. Dr. Brown has ploughed and sown and watered. Please pray that very soon there will be a harvest.

COCHABAMBA, NOVEMBER 1959

This is really a letter from Gordon, although he doesn't yet know it. I am here in Cochabamba having a rather unadventurous time just counting the weeks and days to the arrival of Baby B.

Gordon brought me here and, on the way down, he developed chicken pox and had to stay for nearly three weeks, but he is now back in Alcatuyo working alone. I expect him back here in two weeks time and, when you have read the following, you will understand why I shall be very thankful to see him. I plan to quote excerpts from his letters verbatim.

Monday, 2nd November

Have made a batch of bread. It is a bit heavy and has a strong yeasty taste, but it is edible. The yeast rose but seemed rather sticky. I also put too much sugar in. Then when I went to pump up the stove the pump broke; the end came off the plunger and to get it out I had to disconnect it and remove the whole pump. Got lovely and black. The repairs took an hour, apart from repelling two egg sellers, and by this time the dough was climbing out of the bowl. I did the kneading and cutting in a bit of a hurry, after doing the lunch vegetables. After lunch and huge wash-up felt stonkered, having in fact done less in the morning than my wee wife usually does! Had five minutes siesta, and along came Juandela's lady and little Eberista. Had a 'cuppa' with them and sang some choruses. We killed a garrapata (tick) which was crawling down the leg of the old lady's chair. They said it had come off the cat but I wonder whether it didn't rather come off her clothing. Had cooking fun this evening attempting apple fritters. I got the batter too thin and what little stuck to the apple got blasted off in the eruptions leaving the apple writhing naked in the hot oil!

Saturday, 6th November

Yesterday went quite well. The children behaved very well at midday and the evening meeting was well attended, about twenty I think, with only slight disturbance from outside. I spoke on the parable of the two debtors.

Sunday, 7th November

Come home quickly and save me from the ants!

Thursday, 12th November

Today I have fulfilled an ambition, one that has fascinated me ever since I first saw Alcatuyo a few years ago. I climbed the mountain. As I set out at 6:30 a.m. the weather wasn't very promising, and by the time I got to that great white river bed you can see from here, my goal, the second peak from the right, was hidden from sight in cloud. It was then 8 a.m. and as I climbed, the clouds blew away. That white quebrada (gully) curves away to the right, ending abruptly in a broad amphitheatre, down which water runs from a lagoon perched unexpectedly at the edge on top. That lagoon is the last of a wonderful chain of at least ten, extending North-West up a valley between the two right-hand peaks, and linked by winding water courses and fine cataracts.

I climbed straight up the hillside and along the ridge on the South side of the lagoon and, as I went, the clouds rolled back off the peaks ahead of me. Reaching the crest of the ridge, I found that the mountain was still a long way ahead of me, but it was a rest to walk along the almost level ridge to where the real climb began. Then my legs began to protest and soon it was possible to climb only fifty paces at a time; then my legs would turn to lead, compelling me to sit down and rest on the nearest rock. I reached the visible summit, the one I think you can see from the house, only to find that the highest peak is still further on. Progress was now very slow and in the end, at only 11:30 a.m., I was compelled to sit down and eat my lunch.

The wind was now fresh, but a watery sun warmed up the hillside. The top was now scarcely two hundred yards up. I left the haversack on a prominent patch of bare white earth and clambered to the crest of the ridge. The far side plunged giddily down, down, and then cut away to the Wayc'aya school. I looked up at the peak, a forbidding fifty foot cone of jumbled rock, and began to crawl up. Then suddenly, defeat came. Cramp gripped my legs from hip to toe and, with the cramp, came a wave of giddiness. The majestic scenery on either side changed to a sickening nightmare of vertical space, and I could only lie down in a sandy groove to recover. Actually, I think it might have been dangerous to attempt this last scramble in that state, as a fall down one side would have been some 200 feet, and on any other at least a nasty tumble among the rocks; but the truth is I felt completely drained physically and emotionally. After a while I got back to the haversack, and on the easier down grades the cramp gradually wore off. I think the mountain must approach 15,000 feet. Cramp troubled me most of the way down, and then the nails began to push through my shoes, making walking over rocks and loose stones a misery. I was a wreck for the rest of the evening but am perfectly OK today.

(And he hadn't told anyone where he was going! [Betty])

I had an absurd accident with the car on Wednesday. I went to the Agricultural School, stopped, turned into the gate and, leaving the motor running, went to open the gate. The catch had stuck and I was still fiddling when the lights of the car began to move, and wallop! The front bumper of the car nudged me firmly from behind. I'm still wondering how long and how firmly the car would have continued to push me had the gate remained shut, but it flew open and I scuttled in, shepherded by a gentle Rover. Then I turned and dived for the driver's seat, but the wheels were still turned right and, as I got in the car, it lurched drunkenly round and into the gutter alongside the drive. The lurch coincided with my dive and I hit my head a stunning blow on the top edge of the door, getting a cut that bled a bit. As you can imagine I was still a bit twittery at the beginning of the meeting.

~~~~~~~~~~~~~~~~~~~~~~~~~
~~~~~~~~~~~~~~~~~~~~~~~~~

STOP PRESS Cable sent to Mr. and Mrs. Miles (Betty's parents), (dated 7.12.59)

'MALCOLM GORDON ARRIVED SAFELY TODAY. BETTY WELL. GORDON.'

11
Home with Malcolm

ALCATUYO, MAY 1960

Woe is me! My problem is that I find it impossible to be missionary, housewife, mother and correspondent all rolled into one and something has to go. I am sorry but if I am to be efficient at the first three things the last must suffer. I do so appreciate all the personal letters and would love to write a long reply to each one of you, but I shall have to ask you to be happy with this duplicated one. I thought I was busy before, but now I am just desperate. Gordon and I are both feeling that the altitude is catching up on us insidiously. We get more tired these days and cannot concentrate on vital things. We are not noticeably breathless, but are just listless and disinclined to do anything. I am sure the devil makes full use of the altitude in hindering all the missionaries who try to work here on the Altiplano.

Malcolm is already 5 months old. He is not a placid baby and the high altitude doesn't seem to curtail his activities at all. He is a bundle of energy, feeding well, trying to crawl and making the usual loud baby noises. In fact he does everything pretty well except sleep! We carry him around in a carry-cot which was brought to us from New Zealand. We can hardly move in Potosí for the crowds who follow us around and, if we go into a shop, a crowd gathers at the door. We shocked them one day. We had the carry-cot between us as we went into a shop. I put my side down and Gordon hung on to his! Malcolm rolled out sideways on to the floor and there was a cry of horror from everyone! They, of course, carry their babies safely on their backs. I question the safety when I see mothers, quite drunk, dancing with the baby's poor little head lolling around, and I am sure the kiddie will fall out of the manta. People think Malcolm looks like a little plaster doll and the great fascination is his lack of hair. He has the usual fine down of many European babies, whereas Bolivian babies all have a thick mop of tangled black hair. Malcolm, born completely bald, must have been quite a shock to the old man who assured me (when I was pregnant) that my heartburn was due to the baby's hair being twisted round my stomach!

One thing Malcolm does enjoy is a ride in the car, and sometimes it seems that the worse the road, the better he sleeps in the carry-cot which just fits in the front of the car beside me.

An Indian woman had her eye on our black cat 'Misi' a little while ago. Black cats are considered a very special delicacy! Misi unsuspectingly jumped on the old lady's lap; she felt carefully down his spine and asked, "Is he old?" When we assured her that he was little more than a kitten, she said, "Let me have him when he dies." Poor Misi. That reminds me that we saw the skeleton of a cat hanging on the wall of an Indian home; it was filled with charms of some kind. When Gordon mentioned it the family told us, with self-conscious giggles, what it was. I had gone to the home to treat a boy with a badly injured leg and it necessitated various visits. This was similar to a previous case but fortunately not as bad and much nearer to home. We were able to explain the Gospel to the family on more than one occasion and they listened very well. On a later visit we were amazed to find the house truly 'swept and garnished.' It was clean and tidy and the cat skeleton had been replaced by a Gospel text calendar. We were gladly welcomed, and whether the transformation was for our benefit or not, we do not know. The boy comes to the meeting quite often and the man and his wife came on Friday. We wonder whether or not they will come again.

[This nice young boy was later drowned while we were home on furlough. He had gone to swim in a hot water lake, notorious for a very hot whirlpool. Like others he was sucked into the whirlpool and disappeared. His body was washed up 24 hours later—cooked! We pray he may have understood the Gospel and accepted the Lord as his Saviour before he died.]

Thinking, as I was, of black cats and skeletons brings me to witchcraft, a rather under-the-counter system here, but it is none-the-less real. We had an example of it a week ago. On a routine trip to Puna we came upon a row of blackened cooking pots right across the road and had some difficulty in avoiding them with the car. We thought at first that children had been playing there but, when we saw bits of feathers and tins we suspected witchcraft and hoped it was not directed at us. Ours is about the only car to use that road. Later we were able to ask a young Christian what it was all about. He explained that when someone is ill, the relatives take a sheep and kill it; the entrails and blood are then placed in the pots with other oddments. The belief is that the first person to pass that spot will carry the illness away. We did not become ill. Something very strange happened to the car though and I suspect those pots even now! I am sure there is more demonic power in these things than we like to believe. Certainly the devil seemed to do everything possible to prevent us from getting to Puna. On our next trip everything possible went wrong. The self-starter of the Land Rover wouldn't work, cranking didn't work either; we had two punctures and, without the engine, we could not use the automatic pump, and the foot pump was broken. When at last we limped home, Gordon left the car parked to unload it; the handbrake gave way and the car, with its back door up, ran backwards, full force, into the house wall. The blow dented the back of the car in. Anyway, the house remained intact! Happy days! We went to bed feeling a trifle jaded. All has been put right now though.

We have just had a lovely time with a visitor, Shirley McBride, the latest recruit from New Zealand. She is working in Santa Cruz with the McLeod Smiths. She and Gordon are from the same assembly in New Zealand and hadn't met since he left there seven years ago. Gordon boarded with the McBride family in Auckland for a time, so Shirley's visit was quite an occasion. It was nice for me to have another woman to talk to for a bit and 'Auntie Shirley' was a great help with Malcolm, enabling me to get on with some other things. I am getting to know most of Gordon's friends by name anyway.

Alcatuyo is to have a Government doctor and we are very pleased about it. A newly qualified doctor is to do his year of country service here, and the local folk are building him a house. They started in a wave of enthusiasm but it seems to be waning. At present he is visiting once a week and it is good to be able to send folk to him. A doctor really is needed as we can do very little. To the Indians around us an injection is the cure for everything from a serious disease to a superstition, and they will often not believe that we can treat them. They don't want tablets, only an injection will do! I can clean up injuries but have only embroidery cotton to sew up wounds with, and they tend not to come back to have the stitches out! The medical work has proved to be little help in the missionary work so that we shall not be sorry to be relieved of the responsibility and to have more time for other things.

We do have some laughs about medical things. Once when I was asleep, (siesta time) an Indian woman came to the door and asked Gordon for medicine for her 'wurru.' Gordon hadn't the courage to ask what her 'wurru' might be and, as it seemed she was talking of stomach pain, he gave her a matchbox containing some Epsom salts. After she had gone Fortunata came to me giggling; 'wurru' is the Indian way of saying 'burro' (a donkey)! Gordon had prescribed for the donkey!

A young man, Pablo, came to visit. He, with his wife, had been such a help in the work here, but then he got involved with his father in dubious lawsuits. After a few preliminaries he got down to the reason for his visit. While in the Argentine he had read a book about the 'unforgivable sin' and the doctrine of 'falling away' and it had confused his mind. It left him in such a state of uncertainty and terror lest he had drifted from the Lord with no hope of forgiveness, that he had not slept for a week. Gordon was able to reassure him and show him Scripture verses to indicate that his salvation is 'once for all.' As it says in John 10:28, "...they shall never perish, neither shall any man pluck them out of My hand." He went away a much happier man. We would love to see him with us in the work again.

AUGUST 1960

Well, it looks as though we may soon meet in person. Yes, we are heading for furlough in England. I don't really deserve a furlough yet but Gordon has been here much longer and is feeling in need of a change. I am all for that, but with less reason. Our efficiency seems to be decreasing fast and you will probably find us a bit peculiar! The altitude is said to make us all that way in time! We hope to sail on the 'Reina del Mar' (the boat I came out on) and should arrive, in the Lord's goodness, at Plymouth on the 6th of December.

We expect to leave Alcatuyo at the end of September and have an important assignment in Santa Cruz during the first week of October. Shirley McBride, who visited us a few months back, is to marry Noel McKernon, our friend and fellow worker with whom we stayed in Tupiza. Their paths crossed in Sucre and their love affair was even faster than ours! Santa Cruz is a very long way from here (see map) but we remember how grateful we were to those who travelled a long way, making a special effort for our wedding. I am to be 'Matron of Honour' and Gordon, 'Best Man,' so it will be quite like our own wedding again. (By the way I suspect I am pregnant again so I shall be **very** matronly looking!)

We shall be interested to see the work in the Orient, the tropical lowlands, as it is so different from the work here. There will be no high altitude to worry us, but it will be very hot. I wonder how we shall cope with that. The people are said to be more intelligent there—perhaps we shall be! After our stay in Santa Cruz, we have to go on to Cochabamba to get our documents in order, then up to Oruro by train where we change to the international train to go down to Antofagasta on the coast of Chile. Oh to see the sea! We shall have several days in Antofagasta until the boat arrives from Valparaiso (further South on the coast of Chile) as there is only one train a week. I have seen so many things since I did that train journey up into Bolivia. I wonder how it will seem going down. How wonderful the Lord has been to me even from a purely human point of view. I came out here a single girl feeling that I had sacrificed just about everything, and yet I am coming home with more than I ever thought possible: a husband and a lovely little son. I couldn't believe that the Lord would give me more than I gave up for Him (see Mark 10:29, 30) but He certainly has done 'exceeding abundantly above all that I asked or thought.' Why are we so often slow to trust Him even in these things? Gordon and I are continually proving the Lord's faithfulness and care. We have been very encouraged in the work lately and our only distress is that we cannot do more. We shall look forward to returning from furlough with renewed vigour to carry out several projects that we have in mind.

12
Interlude

Missionary Letters ceased during our furlough as we were once more among relatives and friends, but a few happenings of that time stand out in my mind. I shall never forget the last night of that journey as a frightening storm lashed the boat, or the relief we felt at the sight of Plymouth when we arrived in the early morning and waited out in the bay to go ashore. Sunshine flooded the bay and lit up the green fields beyond the town while an enchanting rainbow added the touch of perfection to the scene. We were home and it was wonderful.

There followed days and weeks and months of reunions with family and friends, and of meeting new friends as we had the joy of making the needs of Bolivia known in new places. We enjoyed meeting missionaries from other lands and comparing notes with them, and we had a most wonderful holiday in Woolacombe, N. Devon, all expenses paid. A very big event of our furlough was the arrival of baby Penelope Joy (Penny) to our family.

MARCH 1961

Let me introduce you to Penelope Joy. She is just three days old. We do praise the Lord for her and for her safe arrival. It has been a real blessing that I was in this country and able to come to the Hospital where I was once a nurse. We would commend our little daughter to your prayers, as a missionary's child life will hold for her, without doubt, some problems and heartaches which are not the normal lot of children in this country. The prospect of having one day to part with our children for their education just doesn't bear thinking about, but "He giveth more grace when the burdens grow greater" so we can leave that in the Lord's hands.

It is good to be home for a while, and we are gradually getting more settled and accustomed to the amenities of civilisation. It is just wonderful to have a hot bath whenever you like, to drink water straight from the tap and to have real milk again. We are fortunate in having a little self-contained flat in my parents' home, and physically we are improving vastly and beginning to feel the benefit of furlough. Even Gordon is a bit fatter and we are all more relaxed. Malcolm is flourishing and is quite the little boy now.

We are getting very booked up with meetings. Gordon will be particularly busy, and I have had many invitations to speak but have, of course, had to refuse them for the moment because of family responsibilities. We would value your prayers that our stay here may be used of the Lord for His glory. It is a tremendous responsibility to put the needs of Bolivia before others. We would not dare to persuade anyone to come to Bolivia but would be thrilled if the Lord were to use us in some way to reveal His will to someone else. Please, would you pray about our home in Alcatuyo? It does need the Lord's care and protection during our absence. I am sure you will remember too the believers we have left behind.

We have been very fortunate to fit two Christmases into our furlough. Our thoughts go back to Bolivia where we last celebrated Christmas with a prized tin of kippers for breakfast, egg and chips for lunch, and some of the top tier of our wedding cake for tea! I can remember the thrill of hearing a little of the 'Nine Lessons and Carols' from King's College on the radio and the Queen's Christmas message. Those times were strange perhaps, but the joy in our hearts was just as real as we remembered the Lord Jesus.

PURLEY, SURREY
DECEMBER 1961

How time flies! When I last wrote Penelope Joy had just made her personal appearance in this world, and now she is a bouncing babe of 9 months. Malcolm is talking a lot now and the two of them keep us very much entertained and very busy. We have so much appreciated the help that many of you have given, often at real cost to yourselves and, as we return to Bolivia, we are sure we can depend on your prayers. That is our greatest need.

We expect to leave a snow-bound England on the 'Reina del Mar' from Liverpool on 28th December. We would especially value your prayers on that day, not only for ourselves but for those we leave behind. The grandparents will not see much of their grand-children growing up, so it is harder for them than for us.

Although there will again be the sadness of saying 'Goodbye' to those we love, it is good to feel that we are on our way back to the place of the Lord's choice for us. We won't see Land's End this time but I am sure that it would look quite different from the way that I saw it when I first left home. Then I felt quite alone, but this time I have the joy of a husband and two lovely children in addition to the Lord's ever present help.

~~~~~~~~~~~~~~

The boat trip should be a relaxation and it is lovely to think we shall soon be back in summer clothes! We are scheduled to arrive in Antofagasta (Chile) on the 26th of January. We then have to wait for the weekly train up into Bolivia, from sea level up to 14,000 feet. Then our problems begin. We do need to purchase a second-hand car, preferably a Land Rover, as soon as we arrive; we hope to find our home in order but it will be a major operation to unpack and make it habitable.
~~~~~~~~~~~~~~

Our first thought will be to find the believers again. Then later, as Dr. and Mrs. Hamilton expect to leave the city of Potosí for health reasons, we have been invited to move in and work there. It will mean an increase in our work load as our present activities will be added to the Potosí work. We shall hope to live in town and do country trips, including Pacasi and Alcatuyo, at intervals. We don't quite know how we shall cope. Dr. Hamilton is very much respected everywhere and there is no way we could attempt to step into his shoes. We shall just have to be ourselves. I expect I shall be writing more about this as time goes on.

Living in Potosí will have some advantages—for example, we shall be able to send and receive mail more frequently (strikes permitting) and there will be a market and shops round the corner. The main disadvantage is that the altitude is more than in Alcatuyo. Please write to us at Casilla 53, Potosí, Bolivia, South America. We leave these shores again, assured that the Lord really has called us to Bolivia and confident that He will go before us.

S.S. REINA DEL MAR
16th JANUARY 1962

This is perhaps the most restful part of our furlough and, although life seems to be full of washing and ironing and baby-minding, we do have some exciting times. I love travelling by boat. The Tourist section of the ship is full of Spanish speaking passengers; I should think 99.9% are Roman Catholics and a fair proportion are priests and nuns, so we are back in the atmosphere of the mission field already. I am trying to write in the lounge but it is full of noisy children who should be in bed!

The early part of the trip was unpleasant. I thought I was a good sailor but I was very unhappy. I'm sure there is nothing more utterly depressing than sea-sickness. However, halfway across the Atlantic things began to improve. The sun came out, the sea calmed, my stomach became my own again and I was able to cheer up!

Our first stop was **Barbados** and we had a really lovely day. After the Spanish ports it had the clean ordered air of a British Possession. It was good to hear English again and to set foot on land once more. In the morning we went into town and browsed around the shops where it seemed possible to buy absolutely anything. In the afternoon we went to a beach to swim. The beach was idyllic: trees gracing the edges of a strip of fine golden sand with corals and shells littered about and a calm turquoise sea. Malcolm and Penny loved the water and had a wonderful time in the sand. Penny must have consumed quite a bit of it as she kept sucking her sandy thumbs! The whole day seemed a rosy dream and we left Barbados to the sound of the oil drum band mingled with the nostalgic 'A Life on the Ocean Wave' played over the ship's loudspeakers. We had seen the luxury of Barbados but we had also seen the little wooden hovels which house the majority of the people in poverty.

La Guayra, **Venezuela**, was, as always, unbearably hot and dirty. We went for a short walk, got diddled by a photographer who produced a quite presentable photograph of us instantaneously, and were heartily thankful to get back to the air-conditioning of the ship. It was interesting to remember that it was here that men boarded the 'Santa María' and later high-jacked her. Venezuelan officials pierced us with their eyes as we returned to the ship. They must have learned to take no chances.

Our day at **Curacao** of the Dutch West Indies was disappointing. Taxis are prohibitive so we walked, and taking a short cut meant a scramble up a cliff face; this was no joke with two pushchairs. Again we did the town in the morning but gave up on the afternoon swim as it would have meant a long trip by taxi. Curacao is an interesting place. The town of Willemstad is thoroughly Dutch and gives the impression that it could have been transplanted from Holland. A pontoon bridge crosses the harbour and it was interesting to see the traffic halted while the bridge was floated back to allow the passage of several large ships as they sailed slowly and majestically to their places at the various wharves. We passed out of the harbour late in the evening when the lights of the city were twinkling on either side, and on into the black night of the sea beyond and so, in about 24 hours, to Jamaica.

Jamaica was another highlight of the voyage. Friends met us here in Kingston and gave us a very happy day. It was Sunday and everyone in Jamaica had a Sunday look. Gordon went to the morning meeting at one of the Brethren Assemblies and had to perspire respectably in a suit and tie. There were about 200 people present. Mr. and Mrs. Foster were so kind to us; their home is delightfully cool and spacious. Malcolm was fascinated to see the lizards scampering on the wall in the garden, especially when one, which Gordon caught in his hand, left its tail there and skidaddled out of sight. In the afternoon Mrs. Wildish, a friend of my mother's, came to tea and it was so nice to see her again. She was very surprised to see me as she had no idea who 'Mrs. Bisset' might be! "Aren't you Betty?" she asked. Mr. and Mrs. Foster took us back to the ship in the evening and we had a little time of prayer together before they left. Such moments are very precious memories.

It was a rough crossing, due south to Cartagena, Columbia. We had a rough day, too. One of our chapters of trouble was that, when we went to the baggage room to get some things from a trunk, we found that a bottle of British Welfare Orange Juice had broken in the trunk. Concentrated Orange Juice is **so** sticky! I brought it with me because Orange Squash is unobtainable in Bolivia and I thought I would use it for the children on train journeys. We had to unpack everything, wash things and even throw some away. The plastic bag the bottle was in saved the worst but it was a horrible mess all the same.

Cartagena, **Columbia**. Today has been unbearably hot and a short walk ashore was all we wanted to see of Cartagena. We have been counting our blessings. Our high altitude is a big problem and wears us out quickly, but we don't have to face intense tropical heat, which is worse. I guess the Lord knows what is best for us.

A wonderful thing that has happened on the voyage is that a young couple have put their trust in the Lord Jesus. They were Roman Catholics, trusting in Sacraments, Confessions and Good Works but, on board ship, things began to happen. They found a Bible in with a life jacket, (who put it there, we wonder?) and it was the beginning of new LIFE for them. A priest confiscated the Bible but the Seed had been sown and they began to make enquiries. Gordon and Mr. Harwood have been able to explain the Way of Salvation to them, and they really do seem to have understood that the only way is by trusting in the Lord Jesus alone, realising that His death on the Cross paid the penalty for their sin, and that in Him they may be forgiven.

~~~~~~~~~~~~~~~~

After Columbia things seemed less exciting. The journey began to feel rather endless in spite of the interest of the **Panama Canal** and other places we visited. Our trips ashore at the various ports were very hot and uncomfortable, and we usually scuttled back to the coolness of the ship as fast as possible, very thankful that the Lord had not called us to serve Him in Columbia or the Canal Zone. After Panama I developed the flu and had to stay in bed with a high temperature and the usual aches and pains. This left poor Gordon with both children all the time and, sensing something was wrong with mother, they were uncooperative. We looked forward to visiting the Somervilles in Lima, but our letter had never arrived and they were not expecting us. Gordon sought them out and they were really pleased to see us so we spent a very happy day with them next day. I was still feeling too wretched to
~~~~~~~~~~~~~~~~

enjoy it very much and the journey to and from their home was difficult; the heat just about flattened us all!

We were really glad when the day dawned on our arrival at **Antofagasta.** Several kind friends on the ship helped me to rush through the laundry I had not been able to do while I was ill and, at last, we were organised and packed and ready to adventure again. Here too, the mail had let us down and our letter about train bookings etc. had not arrived, but we proved how wonderfully the Lord had gone before and prepared the way. The weekly train for Bolivia was to leave next day and although pessimists said, "You'll never get it. You'll have to wait till next week," we did! Our luggage went very smoothly through customs and was up to the station in no time. We changed money to Chilean and Bolivian currency quite easily and our one night in the 'Hotel Splendid' wasn't too bad. We were anxious about whether we would get a sleeper on the train but we needn't have been. The Lord had kept the best one for us! It was larger than the others and had an extra seat and a private toilet. This last was the biggest blessing you can imagine as, in this country, the usual train toilets are unspeakable, (you need to take a large sheet of thick paper for the floor to even tread inside) and by partway through the journey there were so many people in the corridor that we couldn't have got there in any case.

So the first lap of our journey was comparatively comfortable as we sped through the mountainous desert country. We left Antofagasta at 8.45 a.m. on Saturday and arrived at Rio Mulatos (on the Altiplano of **Bolivia**) at 6:30 a.m. the next day. We had to change trains at Rio Mulatos. There was only one First Class carriage (a must for foreigners) and it was full of Quechuas with their bundles of baggage, live chicken etc. All we could find was standing room outside the already revolting toilet; the prospect was grim for a nine hour journey. Just as deep gloom was settling, the Lord sent along something much better. A dining car was added to the train and we were invited to sit in there for the whole journey. It was wonderful. The journey seemed endless and monotonous as we plodded up and over a pass of 15,000FT, said to be the highest railway station in the world.

At last we arrived in Potosí—dirty and dishevelled. All ideas of a last minute wash and brush up and change of clothes had to be abandoned. Gordon just managed to shave at the entrance to the dining car, with a mugful of hot water balanced on the pushchair and no mirror! Dr. and Mrs. Hamilton were waiting at the station, complete with a large crowd of believers who had come straight from Sunday School to meet us. We were overwhelmed at the welcome and were glad to reach the Hamilton's flat.

Everything is so much the same that it hardly seems we have been away, and here we are temporarily installed in the room behind the Hall. Things have been going smoothly and we have been conscious of the Lord's help. Customs Officers opened only one box and were very good to us and the Police seemed quite content to have us back! Gordon has had to go through all the fingerprint business again as his identity card had expired. One sticky snag—literally—cropped up as one of our boxes began to ooze a river of sticky sweetness. Who suggested we should bring Golden Syrup? Two 2lb tins had emptied their contents into a box of new woollies. It took us all day to clean up the mess. We rescued some things but have a bagful of sticky woollies to deal with later.

Our problems now concern shopping. Gasoline is almost unobtainable and we need it for our cooking stove. We can't find any sugar and other things are scarce. We hoped to get to Alcatuyo on Friday but it looks as though we must wait until after the weekend. We shall have to hire a lorry to get us all, plus baggage, there as so far we have no car.

13
Home Again

ALCATUYO, FEBRUARY 1962

The Lord undertook for us wonderfully on our journey back, and we continually saw instances of His care and provision for us. On the Saturday after our arrival in Potosi we managed to get a truck to take us and our luggage home to Alcatuyo. While loading the truck we discovered that our tape-recorder had been stolen from us. Dr. Hamilton had been using it for his radio programmes while we were away and gave it back the night before we left. Someone must have seen it while the door was open; we hadn't thought to hide it. We brought with us a small transistor set to use in conjunction with the big one, so we shall have to make do with that. The idea was to take the small transistor set into Indian homes, meetings etc. where there is no electricity, and then to transfer and edit our recordings on to the bigger recorder. Notices about it are being broadcast on the radio and other missionaries informed. It is probably the only one of its kind in the country.

Very stiff from the journey and with some trepidation we first sighted the house, our home. A ditch had to be filled and a wall knocked down before the truck could get to the house. Everything seemed to be in good order, though there were some signs of flooding especially in the kitchen. Our furniture was all just as we left it, and once the thick but superficial dust was swept away, the place was quickly habitable and within a week was back in its usual running order. I had been so worried lest Fortunata should have married or gone away as nothing had been heard of her for about six months. I must say a lump came into my throat as she came hurrying across from her house within a few minutes of our arrival. She had been faithfully sleeping in the one room open to her and generally caring for the property. How good the Lord is!

The altitude bothered us quite a bit at first and neither of us felt well for the first two weeks here. We seem now to have got accustomed to it and it is nice to feel ourselves again. Almost immediately we lost all the weight we had put on while on furlough, but we are both feeling better now than we have done for a long while. Perhaps this is because the children are settling in well and we are at last getting more sleep.

We are very hampered in the work so far in that we have no car. This is an urgent matter for prayer that the Lord would find one for us very soon so that we are able to visit Puna and the other places around. In the meantime we have tried to get out walking and visiting the homes around us. We have been generally well received and, as a result, several strangers came to the meeting last night. I wish you could have seen them. The room was just about full with twenty-three present, and probably half of these had not heard the Gospel before, certainly not from us. We wonder how much they understood. It is almost Carnival time, when sin will abound, and these are the folk who…'sit in darkness and the shadow of death.' How we long for the privilege of seeing them illumined by…'the light of the knowledge of the glory of God in the face of Jesus Christ.'

~~~~~~~~~~~~~~~~~~~~

The other day, when Gordon was away in Potosí, there was a terrific hail storm. The sky was dark and I gradually became conscious of an uncanny caterwauling outside. I thought at first that it was the schoolboys yelling over a football match, but then it seemed to come from somewhere nearer than the school so I went outside. In the fields all around women were wailing at the skies:
~~~~~~~~~~~~~~~~~~~~

hail was obviously coming and this is harvest time. They were throwing something into the air and I couldn't catch their words as they wailed. Fortunata told me it was—

> 'Pasay pasay suwa, tarapachaman pasay'
> (Pass, pass thief, to the desert pass)

They lit fires everywhere till the fields were covered with smoke and they exploded dynamite (that is what they were throwing into the air). They were also sounding a deep kind of horn, a waca wajra (cow's horn). There was general panic all round. I got a little of the wailing on a tape but was really too late for much and Malcolm kept talking. The hail came in spite of it all, easily the size of marbles and in no time our patio was deep in it. It did a lot of damage to the crops.

Two of the schoolmasters come over here quite a lot. They seem nice young fellows though I am a bit afraid of them. I think they like me too much! They asked if I would give them meals as they have no one to cook for them! That would be a new job—school canteen cook! I was amused that they asked. They must have liked the tea and supper they had as guests.

~~~~~~~~~~~~~~~~~~~~~

Dr. and Mrs. Hamilton expect to move to the Argentine as soon as the political situation has quietened down. They have asked us to move into Potosí when they have gone, to carry on the work there. They have offered us their car, and we shall probably be living in their flat as a temporary measure. The Hamiltons have lived there 'temporarily' for sixteen years! They have never found anything better. At least it has running water, a proper sink in the kitchen and a civilised toilet. It even has an enormous bath, but the bathroom is vast and very cold and I am not sure whether we shall have the courage to get into the bath. It has no hot water so we would have to carry that through to the bath after heating it on the cooker. I wish we could take Fortunata as she knows our ways and
~~~~~~~~~~~~~~~~~~~~~

is very good with the children, but I shall have to have a Spanish speaking girl. There will be meetings almost every night, some afternoons, and all day on Sundays so we shall be very busy. I am sure that we shall sometimes flee here to Alcatuyo for refuge. We shall be really sorry to leave Alcatuyo, but the text on our calendar this morning was a help to us. It said 'If Thy presence go not with us carry us not up hence…My presence will go with thee and I will give thee rest.' We do really feel that the Lord is with us in this. I shall enjoy having a class of teen-age girls and we are feeling quite enthusiastic about our new type of work. Town life will be very different; it won't be such fun for the children I'm afraid. There is a large terrace where they will be able to play, but it will not seem much after the wide open spaces of Alcatuyo.

POTOSI, JUNE 1962

We had settled happily into our home and work in Alcatuyo and were a bit desperate because we had no car. We were so encouraged with the work there. Often our little Hall was packed out with thirty or so people with perhaps only two of them believers. Five of the schoolteachers began to come to meetings and showed a really intelligent interest. You could have heard a pin drop as they listened to the testimony on tape of Luis Montaña, 'The Monk who lived again' (perhaps you have read the book). He was a Bolivian priest who escaped from a monastery in Peru and ran to the 'foreign devil' asking, "Tell me if you have peace in your heart." One of the teachers, Alfredo, professed to be saved. His home is in Puna and he could, if he goes on, be such a help to the little church there.

Gordon frequently had to waste so much time waiting for trucks to bring him into town for our supplies…or was it a waste of time? Sometimes it seemed so and at other times we felt the Lord had a purpose in it, especially when a priest gave him a lift and he was able to speak about the Gospel to him, or when the other passengers on top of a truck were willing to listen for a time and accept tracts. All the same we were glad when the Lord answered our prayers and we were able to purchase a vehicle for ourselves. We bought it from Dr. Hamilton so it has always been 'in the work.' It is a 1951 Dodge ¾ ton truck, a rather old one and perhaps not what we would have chosen, but very well cared for and roadworthy.

So here we are at last, city dwellers again. Gordon came up with the luggage on Monday/Tuesday, and on Wednesday we all came, complete with Fortunata. We had a picnic lunch on the way. We settled into the room behind the Hall and prepared to make the best of it for a night. That evening there was a Farewell Meeting for the Hamiltons with refreshments afterwards. A crowd of women came to prepare the refreshments, bringing hordes of children with them. All the children gazed at Malcolm and Penny who promptly began to show off; they were thoroughly excited by bedtime. I eventually got Penny to sleep, but Malcolm came to the meeting in his dressing gown and slept in Gordon's arms. It was a lovely meeting, and afterwards we were served with cocoa and some doubtful looking cakes and biscuits.

Dr. and Mrs. Hamilton left next morning and we moved into their flat. The Assembly have given us a wonderful welcome here. We enjoyed the meeting on Sunday morning but, Sunday School was pandemonium as I had to take our children with me. They are really too young and were playing and fighting round me as I tried to speak to the girls.

A car is not the only thing we have inherited from the Hamiltons! We have stepped into their flat, much of their furniture, and their responsibilities in the Assembly. We feel very inadequate as they were such excellent missionaries and were loved by all the townspeople, whether Christians or not. Everyone regrets their going, but they have also given us a very warm welcome indeed. This is obviously the more strategic centre and we are now alone in a vast area. Only Dr. and Mrs. Brown and ourselves remain as

Quechua-speaking Assembly workers. Gordon and I are only beginners. How much we need some new workers. One day last week we visited Pacasi for the day and it almost broke our hearts to see all that Dr. Hamilton had to leave there: a presentable house, a good meeting hall and medical rooms well equipped with instruments and medicines. All is ready for a doctor to walk in and begin, but there is no doctor!

As to Assembly responsibilities, there are four groups here in Potosí: one Spanish and three Quechua-speaking. There is an Assembly in Pacasi, one in Puna, and a few believers in Alcatuyo and in other scattered villages. We hope to visit them all and to continue preaching in the various village fairs as well. This will mean a lot of travelling, packing and unpacking. We help in the activities of the main Assembly here but the organising is done by the local church elders. Gordon is responsible for the Sunday evening Gospel meeting and the ministry on Friday, and he has a class of adults at Sunday School. He also takes a turn at preaching in the other three halls, speaking in Quechua. I have a teenage class in Sunday School and help with the various women's meetings. On Wednesday evenings I play the harmonium for the meeting while Gordon takes a turn at baby-sitting for a change! This adds up to a full time job for me as I need to do so much preparation for talks, and spontaneous prayer in either language is agonising. Hopefully I shall become more confident with experience.

After the meeting on Sunday three people professed to be saved, and another in one of the Quechua halls. One was a young man we have spoken to in Alcatuyo, and his conversion came rather through those conversations. Two were teenagers and the other a lady whose husband was saved some time ago. We have much for which to praise God. One of the first things we had to cope with was rather interesting. About a dozen Indian Christians from an isolated village came to town. They complained of persecution from the authorities to the extent of being beaten up and threatened with death. Gordon and two other Christians from here went with them to the police. They were given a very strong letter of reprimand to the 'mayor' of the village and, since he is likely to be hauled over the coals if it happens again, all should be well. The Indians went off very happily with their letter (which none of them could read!) and Gordon had the privilege of reading to them some of the Lord's words about persecution.

We are still feeling the altitude quite a lot. We always seem to be tired and cannot hurry around. We have colds and I suffer from masses of tiny little cracks in my fingers. I find it hard to do up and undo buttons and holding a pen is miserably painful. It is very cold, my skin seems to dry up and layers of cream seem to make little difference.

My mother, in England, is very unwell. After several weeks in hospital she is home but will have to take things very quietly. It makes it hard to be so far away, especially as I am her 'one and only.' I do trust her to the Lord. He knows all about her.

14
Adventures, Misadventures or Camping with the Kids!

POTOSI 1962

I hardly know what to call this chapter! It all happened on a trip to Cochabamba to a Worker's Conference last month. We decided to go all the way by car, a three day journey. We were especially keen to try out the inflatable 'Igloo' tent we had brought back with us from England. We had not heard of anyone using one before and were anxious to discover whether it was suitable for use in this country.

We set out from Potosí in fine style (five minutes before schedule!) aiming for Sucre and the home of Dr. and Mrs. Brown, to spend Sunday with them. The morning went well and we stopped for lunch in a pleasant but sandy spot on a very high plateau; then began the long descent into the valley of the Pilcomayo River. The road was the usual precipitous hairpin variety so we took it pretty cautiously. Rounding a bend we suddenly came upon a truck completely overturned right across the road! The two occupants had just managed to crawl out; the driver was unhurt, but his companion obviously had a broken arm. The driver was a young man known to Gordon, son of one of the Christians in Sucre. They were fortunate to have escaped death as only a short distance further would have taken the vehicle over the edge to a tremendous drop. We did all we could for the injured man; he sat in our camp chair in what little shade our car afforded. I splinted his arm with a roll of tracts (I wonder what happened to them in the hospital later), bound it with one of Penny's nappies (diapers) and a patriotic Bolivian ribbon, and then made a sling with another nappy. We were held up for nearly two hours until enough man power turned up to push the upturned vehicle to one side so that we could pass. We took the injured man in the back of our car and went on our way a trifle shaken.

It seemed a long time before the Pilcomayo came in sight. The bridge is broken; a driver had insisted on driving too heavy a vehicle over it so the bridge collapsed, the truck dropped far below into the river, and both the driver and his mate were killed. The bridge looked frighteningly pathetic hanging on along one edge and now there is no alternative but to ford the river. We pondered the situation, watched another vehicle go through (we learned later that it had a four wheel drive, we didn't!) and decided it didn't look too bad. We edged bravely in. By the time we were halfway across the water was up to the door and the engine went phut! With a grimace of despair Gordon took off his shoes, rolled up his trouser legs and got out. As he opened the door and stepped down, the water was up to his thighs and a tidal wave swept through the cab. Malcolm was excited! "Daddy's in the water!" and Penny was leaning out trying to touch it so that I had my hands full trying to hold them both. At last, after about half an hour's tinkering, and with the help of two other men from a passing truck, the engine spluttered into life. It was never quite the same again and had little power as we limped the rest of the way to Sucre. It was well after dark when we arrived, but then we had to find the owner of the truck and tell him about the accident, leaving the injured man with him. The Brown's house is about half-an-hour out of town; in the pitch dark night we lost our way and were wandering for about an hour until we found the right track to the house.

Monday's journey took us along the valleys of the Rio Chico and then the Rio Grande. We began to appreciate what the hymn writer meant when he wrote about 'a shelter from the noontide heat and the burden of the day.' We were aiming to reach a place called Aiquile. The children were very restless in the car and as the road continued to hairpin perilously, I got desperately tired with the effort of swinging their bodies around the bends as well as my own. We made an unsuccessful detour to help a truck in distress, lost time and got hotter than ever and the children were filthy from playing in the dust. Our hopes of reaching Aiquile faded and, having found a suitable site to pitch the tent, we decided to stop.

The tent was erected in no time and I soon washed up picnic things and got a meal ready. The only snag was the dust; we and all our belongings were covered. Soon after dark we were tucked up in sleeping bags on airbeds. We shared our camping ground with two or three herds of llamas and their llameros; the light of their fires was quite a comfort to us during the night. We had been so hot during the day that we imagined the night would be mild. We were wrong! It was dreadfully cold and until the sunshine came over the mountains and down the valley we were frozen. The children were cross and crying just because of the cold and we couldn't persuade them to stay in the tent. Breakfast was a chilly meal and packing up difficult, but at last we were on our way and were soon too hot again.

The main hazard of the day was the descent into the Misqu'i valley and a tremendous climb up the other side. We must have been climbing through a series of hairpin bends for about an hour. I dared not look down. There wasn't so much as an inch of parapet to protect us from a drop of something like 2,000 feet. The radiator boiled and we felt pretty drained ourselves by the time we reached the top. From then on things went smoothly till we were about nine miles from Cochabamba, where we were stopped at a police barrier and the gear stuck in neutral! The car would not budge in spite of considerable coercion. Just then a bus came in sight, so I grabbed a bit of money and the children and caught the bus, leaving Gordon to don overalls and get under the car. The bus was already more than full; someone took Penny out of my arms and I lost sight of her. Malcolm, standing beside me was just about smothered by the very full polleras (skirts) of the ladies but he didn't complain. By much compression, an inch or two of seat was found for me and we were soon disgorged at the market in Cochabamba. I took a taxi to the HQ of the Bolivian Indian Mission, where we were fed and cared for. A kind missionary friend set out to rescue Gordon. The friend eventually pushed our car with his for some distance (towing is forbidden) and it slipped into gear again. From then on it behaved very well. We were late arriving at the BIM School where the conference was to be held, and most of our fellow missionaries were there to greet us. When Gordon walked in there was a momentary silence and then a roar of laughter! It is difficult to explain how dreadful he looked!

The conference was a wonderful time for refreshment and blessing. We enjoyed it all and felt it was definitely worthwhile. We studied the Epistle to the Philippians in the morning and the First Epistle of John at night, and many practical problems were sorted out in the business sessions. It was wonderful to meet so many fellow workers again, too.

The journey home had its moments, starting with a minor mishap when we met a truck on a bend. The truck was much too near the middle of the road and, since we had the outside of the bend and a steep drop below us, we were keeping as far from the edge as possible with the result that the truck shaved off our door handle and mirror and scuttled off without any word of apology. That night we found a wonderful camping spot, and as we were getting really experienced at unpacking and repacking, our troubles seemed somewhat diminished.

The next day we got stuck in the mud by some road works and had to be hauled out by a bulldozer. We got right on past Sucre and down to the Pilcomayo River again. This time we took all precautions removing the fan belt and covering the engine and, with a fervent prayer, the Lord got us safely through; we camped for the night on the other side. We wondered why people didn't come to watch us camping as they are usually so inquisitive about the strange foreigners. We decided it must be because the ghostly green tent with the light inside frightened them. Our children were great fun, romping around in the evening and 'helping' by such things as pouring water into the gasoline for the cooking stove. In the morning they were too cold to care. We arrived home in Potosí quite early, with time to unpack and organise ourselves before bed. We were so thankful to the Lord for bringing us home safely.

~~~~~~~~~~~~~~~~~~

A country trip took us through Alcatuyo and Pacasi for a few days, and our journey home could have ended in tragedy. The road home took us through a village called Chaquí; we stopped there to preach as there was a big fair in progress. Gordon went off to preach and I was left guarding the luggage, the car and the children. It was the usual rowdy, revolting fair! Drunken men were lying in their own vomit, people's fiesta clothes were looking the worse for the revelry; there were animals for sale and Indian bands with drunken dancers. The children were awfully good, standing and watching everything.

One of the main activities seemed to be that half-drunken men and boys charge through the crowd on galloping mules. Penny all but went under the hoofs of one of them but, in the Lord's goodness, all was well. I was petrified with fright as I saw her toddle into the path of the mule, and all the people around gasped with horror as the galloping mule charged towards her. I think the mule itself avoided her as the rider was incapable (though he turned and swore at me like anything!) I trembled for hours. I had been watching her so carefully but, just at that second, took my eyes off her, noticing that Gordon was coming back with an unknown man. The man was trying to extort an unjust fine out of Gordon and he was rightly refusing to pay. We suspect he was trying to
~~~~~~~~~~~~~~~~~~

'put it across' the gringos, (foreigners) and he went off. We also suspect he was drunk.

After that, and still trembling, we did a good deed and passed current from our car battery to another vehicle. They must have done something funny to our engine as, when we continued on our way, it began to play up. It had been running so smoothly, and from that moment things began to go wrong. It began to 'ping' all the time, we lost oil and the radiator boiled. I got a picnic tea while Gordon tinkered with the car. He got it back into reasonable order and, once it started, we jumped in and began to limp uncertainly back home. About twenty minutes later Gordon suddenly said, "My jacket!" He had left it by the roadside and a teddy bear and sunhat were with it. We were so anxious listening to the motor that we had just driven off without checking. We went all the way back but, of course, all had disappeared. The jacket pockets contained our house keys (a neighbour later showed us how to get in through a fanlight!), post office box key, a bit of cash, Gordon's driving licence and certificate of ownership of the car. We had brought home my treadle sewing machine and the Indian who carried it in for us broke a piece off the polished top. It was the last straw. What a day! It is trips like these that drain all our physical, mental and spiritual energy. Never mind. We are in the Lord's hands. We hoped that some honest soul would bring the jacket back. *They didn't! All had to be replaced.*

~~~~~~~~~~~~~~~~~~~~~~

We were much encouraged here in Potosí when, last month, fifteen were baptised. Some were from the city of Potosí itself and others from the country around, some of them were folk we had seen saved ourselves and others were from before our time here. The baptism was held in the patio of the home of one of the elders of the Assembly, and it was crowded. Gordon and one of the elders shared the baptising and the other two spoke briefly, one in
~~~~~~~~~~~~~~~~~~~~~~

Spanish and the other in Quechua. Do pray for these folk and praise the Lord for them.

On a visit to Alcatuyo recently we were thrilled to find the school teacher, Alfredo, going on well as a Christian. He has no one there to help him, but he studies the Bible and is obviously growing in the faith. He is really interested in winning others and is even contemplating doing some preaching himself in Puna. He does need your prayers for we are sure the devil will not leave him alone if he is an effective witness. One day, while we were there he arranged a meeting for Gordon at another school. He sent a telegram to the school but it never arrived (typical!) so no one came to the meeting, but they did have a very interesting time with the school master and his wife there, speaking about the gospel. They really felt it was worth while and Alfredo was thrilled to bits.

The class we have for girls on Saturday evenings is proving quite a success and, so far, seven new girls have been, and some come again. We are not sure whether to invite boys as well; this could cause problems in this country, but other groups do it and thereby attract some of our young people. The trouble is that we have so much more to do than we can adequately cope with. So many of the believers in the district are crying out for us to visit them and we just cannot do it. We feel that the work here in town is suffering because we have to be away so often. At present we are immersed in repairs on the Alcatuyo house and are experiencing endless frustrations in that. There is more than enough for us to do in the city alone and, much as we love the country work, things would go much better if the Lord would send someone else to help with that. There is a missionary house vacant in Alcatuyo and another in Pacasi. It would be no easy task for new workers as it would mean learning Spanish first and then Quechua and living in quite primitive conditions, but it can be done. With the Lord's help we have proved it. We love Alcatuyo and would go back there like a shot but we feel the Lord has called us here now and the city is the obvious strategic place to be. Please ask the Lord to call someone else to this region of Bolivia.

15
Town and Country Troubles

MARCH 1963

TOWN—House hunting is such a slow business! We heard of a likely one in answer to our radio notice, a chalet type of house, almost English looking, but it wasn't any good. The rooms were light and attractive, but there were not enough of them. The kitchen was a dark little hole and the toilet on the other side of the 'garden.' There was no protection from burglars and, anyway, it was too far out of town for us. Then we heard of another which sounded quite hopeful and we are going to see it on Monday. We have seen the outside but it looks far too small. It is only half finished and promises to be very nice. It would be nice to have somewhere new and therefore clean and fresh, but it is so tiny I'm afraid our furniture would never fit in it. We have been walking the streets looking for somewhere suitable and knocking on doors, but with no success so far. There is a ray of hope for tomorrow though. While we were out we met the lady who sold us the Land Rover and she said "I know someone who has an apartment you could have; it is very nice and has a bathroom." We nearly jumped for joy. She told us to look for the owner in a certain stationery shop, so we trotted off there straight away. Oh! It was Saturday afternoon and the shop was closed! We shall follow the lead first thing on Monday morning. The Land Rover lady has a lovely home herself and is likely to know what kind of thing we are looking for, and she even has a beautiful bathroom. She said we could use her name. We mustn't get too excited though as we are so often disappointed. The Lord has it all under control and we are sure that He has the right place for us somewhere. We are not looking for luxury but we do need a degree of 'modern conveniences' to be able to work efficiently and to entertain missionary visitors.

We shall probably be renting a place, but there is another interesting way of 'renting' a home which we may have to use. You pay a lump sum for perhaps two years and then live rent free. If, after that time, you buy the place the lump sun goes towards it. If you do not buy it you get the original sum back after the set time. It is rather like lending money with the house as guarantee. The owner will probably invest the money or use it for some project. You just have to hope and pray that, when the time comes to hand it back, he hasn't lost it!

We are desperate because of a shortage of water. There has been no more than a drip in the tap for days and often none at all. We are down to our last drop tonight. There is just enough for coffee tonight and tea in the morning, and we have guests staying with us too. How important water is to us all! We are hoping and praying there will be some in the tap tomorrow.

~~~~~~~~~~~~~~~~

Great excitement! We have decided on the house we thought would be too small. We saw it this morning and, although it is indeed very small, I think we can arrange it suitably, so we have agreed to take it. It has many advantages in being brand new and, as it isn't yet complete, we can have a say in how we want it. It is a bit difficult having the staircase half outside, but that is quite common in this country. At least we have a whole house to ourselves, and it has a nice balcony which I can make pretty with plants. We shall be conveniently near to the Hall, market and
~~~~~~~~~~~~~~~~

shops, only a minute or two to each, and the front door is right on to the street. In Bolivia each householder has to have the street in front of his house swept by 8 a.m. This is an excellent rule, as you would agree if you could see the day's accumulation of rubbish in the street!

NOVEMBER 1963

We are feeling frantically impatient about the lovely little house the Lord has provided for us. We do thank Him for it and know that in His good time we shall be in it, but we are up against the inevitable South American 'mañana' (tomorrow) mentality. The owner is a charming man, a lawyer, but he just doesn't get things done. He promised the house for October 30th, then November 30th, and now we begin to doubt that. We are praying that we shall be settled in by the end of November. December is such a busy month getting everything organised for the New Year activities which are very important here. There are prizes all round, 800 bags of sweets to prepare, and all the recitations etc. to rehearse to perfection for THE day, and we do need our minds free for all this. It would be awful to have to move house in the midst of it.

Some time later…

We hope to move in at the end of this week! The front door is ready and would do credit to a prison! It is a tremendously thick wooden door with a studded iron plate covering it completely. It should be secure against a tank! We shall have to get a ladder to keep upstairs as a fire escape as the only way out is via the front door. Fires are uncommon in this country, (there is no Fire Brigade) but it is as well to be prepared as we use so much gasoline in the house. We are regretting that we never did, as we intended, bring a light ladder from England.

DECEMBER 1963

I have just heard with dismay that my last Prayer Letter never turned up. I wrote with some urgent items for prayer, and in some of our more depressed moments we have comforted ourselves with the thought that 'the folk at home will be praying anyway.' The devil seems to be doing his utmost to hinder us at the moment and I have my suspicions that he intercepted that letter. Gordon suggested that we should 'register' this one with prayer to thwart his plans this time.

Gordon has been rushing around looking for workmen, cement, glass for the windows, and then rushing to the Hall to rehearse the children for their recitations etc. All this is a tremendous strain at this altitude, where you can't even think straight! We have had to waste so much time doing things that were really the responsibility of others. At last we have two Christians working on the house and it has made a considerable difference this past week.

~~~~~~~~~~~~~~~

COUNTRY—(Alcatuyo again) Various factors contribute to our extreme tiredness just at the moment. One is the housework. My wonderful helper, Fortunata, is ill, quite seriously ill I think, so she hasn't been able to work for us this time. She may be pregnant but has been having rigors and a lot of pain in her back. I've managed (with the Lord's help) to pull her together with penicillin and she is up now but still far from well. I really miss her, for herself as well as for the work she does. Juana's little girl, Grecencia, has been coming to help me. She is a good little thing, only about 12 years old but she is pretty capable and quick to learn. We like her and shall probably keep her on while we are here, and she tells me that she likes coming. Just now though, she is only learning and is slow, so I have to do a lot of housework myself. I've been washing (by hand), ironing and cleaning and it has served to remind me
~~~~~~~~~~~~~~~

that I am a foreigner and cannot do it at this altitude. I'm rushing around all day and now have a headache every afternoon and an ache around my ribs.

Our bedroom roof was in danger of falling in so we have had to have the whole roof off that room! We have all the bedroom furniture in the dining room and the bedroom itself is open to the skies; with one delay after another we begin to wonder if we shall ever have a roof on again. The workmen are quite unintelligent about the work and seem all out to deceive us, trading on our ignorance of the job in hand. One of the beams had broken through and the whole side was sagging badly. Here, over the main framework, they put a frame of canes tied together, then a layer of mud, and then the tiles fit into that. The joins are then filled with cement. The walls are falling outwards with the weight of the roof and have to be 'tied' together with an iron rod right through the room—so attractive!

So, Gordon is weary of workmen and I am weary of housework, and today there has been a fair in Belén to which we felt compelled to go and preach the Gospel. We all went this morning and, while I trotted the children round the fair, Gordon joined the believers to preach. We excused ourselves and hurried home to lunch to avoid self-invited guests, then Gordon went back to carry on. At 3 p.m. we had a Breaking of Bread meeting in our kitchen with fourteen of us present. After the meeting I gave them all tea and bread. For one awful moment we thought one family had elected to stay to supper and for the night, but we managed to persuade them that it wasn't really worth it as there would not be an evening meeting. I know I should be 'given to hospitality' and I do try to be, but that particular family have an uncanny knack of turning up at mealtimes and sitting still until fed! They are difficult to entertain too as they contribute nothing to the conversation; their spiritual progress is an encouragement to us though.

Really this visit has become a bit of a nightmare. The roof is nearly finished but the men have just decided that they need 200 more new tiles, so we have to search for them tomorrow. Whether they will finish in time for us to clean the room and put the furniture back remains to be seen. We really must as the Browns are coming here for a visit and, since this is their house, we can't let them arrive to chaos!

I have been slogging at housework all day as even Grecencia has failed to turn up. I think her unsympathetic father must have clamped down on her coming. For three days we have had no help at all. Yesterday, to crown it all, the pump broke! Gordon spent half the day hacking it out of the wall where it was cemented in, and we shall have to take it to Potosí for repair. We really need a new one but we have never seen one for sale. Gordon has been water boy for two days. He has to carry buckets right round the house, take the wire netting off the front of the well, and let down a jug on a long line—a slow laborious process. The water is dirty too, as dirt from the sides of the well falls into it on the way up, there being no proper pulley system. Never mind, we still have water and that is really something to be thankful for. Today has been brighter so I did the washing outside with the children paddling around in bathing trunks. It gave quite a holiday air to the whole thing and lightened the burden considerably.

My hands are suffering from the altitude. My fingers have lots of tiny cracks and it really hurts to do up or undo buttons etc., and it makes it very painful to write or even type. Layers of cream make no difference. My lower lip gets a deep crack down the centre too and it is so difficult to get it to heal.

~~~~~~~~~~~~~~~~~~~

POTOSI

It's Christmas, but it doesn't feel the least bit like it and we are even in danger of forgetting the day! The weather is horrid…the
~~~~~~~~~~~~~~~~~~~

sun usually shines in the morning but torrents of rain fall in the afternoons, often with storms. There is nothing Christmassy about the shops (except for some scenes of Bethlehem in shop windows here and there) and it feels all wrong. One needs dark evenings and carols and pretty lights. We have had a few Christmas cards in the mail and each one gives us quite a jolt. I meant to make a cake but haven't had the ingredients or the time; anyway, the true remembrance of the Lord's birth will be just as real without all the frills. The children will have a pile of presents. Yesterday I went into a shop in what we call 'Bond Street' as it is the poshest shopping street in Potosí. They had crystallised fruit and big boxes of English chocolates, (at a price!) and the lady gave Penny a bar of Cadbury's chocolate. As we came out a raucous loudspeaker was blaring out carols and for a moment a bad twinge of homesickness got me.

I wonder whether we shall remember to get anything for each other! We forgot our Wedding Anniversary till we looked at the calendar that day and decided that the 15th November sounded familiar! I was thinking though, just this evening, how happy we all are. I am so glad that I obeyed the Lord and came here to Bolivia when He called me, even though it was hard at the time. He certainly multiplied the blessings. I thought I was giving up everything but really He was waiting to *give* me everything. When I look back I wonder how I ever did it at all; for years it was just a nebulous dream and, in spite of all my brave talk, I didn't in my heart expect to ever get here! It was the biggest surprise of my life that the Lord let me go through with it. Looking back I shudder to remember the agonies...saying 'Goodbye' and often crying myself to sleep, especially on the boat but even into Tupiza days. Yet how wonderful the Lord has been and here I am, happily married and with two lovely children and, above all, a real work to do for the Lord. I'm not a very splendid missionary, especially lately, as we have been so preoccupied with all the house problems. Do pray that in the New Year we may really give our whole hearts and minds to the Lord's work again. We hope to spend a morning together in prayer each week, do a lot of visiting, more language study and Bible study, and get out into the country work again. No doubt the devil will try to upset our plans.

We are thrilled at the way the young people's work is growing. The girls continue to come and sometimes bring others; they obviously enjoy it. We began with four boys and last night there were seven. If all came together there could be twenty to twenty five.

Malcolm and Penny do love music. The moment there is a squeak from the record player, they rush for chairs to stand on to get as close as they can. Malcolm listened to records for hours this afternoon. He specially loves 'Laughing Ginger Brown' and the Farmyard noises on the flip side, but he is also very fond of the Vienna Boys' Choir. Malcolm always talks of playing the 'pinanno' one day.

CALLE INGAVI, POTOSI,
JANUARY 1963

Believe it or not, but here we really truly are in our new house! I can't say we are exactly comfortable, but we have bright hopes for the future.

Tuesday was New Year's Day, of course. We were so relieved that all went wonderfully, a real answer to prayer. We were thrilled that the general impression seemed to be that the children's programme was at least as good as usual. Don Juan, one of the elders, gave his opinion as "Magnífico!" You can guess what that means. The recitations and hymns went off very well; I do wish you could have heard them. I was near to tears as I always am on a momentous occasion. All seemed satisfied with their prizes and bags of sweets. We were all dressed up in our best clothes for the occasion. Penny wouldn't sit still and kept going between Gordon's legs while he was speaking. It was so funny for the audience to see frilly pants disappearing between his knees and then a naughty little face peeping back again to assess the effect!

The actual house move went very smoothly. Of the two young girls who help me in the house, Valeriana stayed in the old one and cleaned up as things were taken away, and Dominga and I went to the new house. An older girl, Lucia, took the children out for the two days. We slept at the house on Friday night, though poor Gordon nearly didn't! He was exhausted and I had been really worried about him shifting so much heavy stuff...we were ready for bed and there was a knock at the door. Oh no! Here I must digress and tell you another story...

Have I told you before about a Christian lady who asked us to go to her house where her husband, sister and brother-in-law all wanted to be saved, and they wanted to dedicate their truck to the Lord? We went with her to the tidy adobe house and there, sure enough, were all the folk concerned, all of Chola (mixed race) class. We had a time of prayer and explained the way of Salvation but they evidently had it all thought out beforehand and were truly converted. There was great rejoicing in that household (and in heaven) over three of them saved that day. (We did pray about the truck too. It had previously been dedicated to the Virgin and we had to explain that praying was not like a good luck charm).

It was some months later when that same Christian lady knocked on the door. This time the lady was in tears. The traffic authorities had received a telegram to say that her brother-in-law's truck had overturned over the bank and four were killed. She didn't know whether her relatives were killed or not so please would Gordon take her there to see. Our hearts sank to rock bottom. The truck was in a place called Tinkipaya, accessed by a renownedly dangerous road; it was dark and Gordon was dead tired and therefore not in a fit state to drive safely. Eventually Gordon went off to find out more from the traffic police, while I tried to comfort the lady and pray with her in a mixture of Spanish and Quechua. By this time a list of the dead had been received, not including the brother-in-law and his wife, so Gordon agreed to go early next morning to see if he could help. After a few hours of sleep he set off, appalled at the state of the road and very thankful he had not attempted the trip in the night.

The truck was in a river bed, on its wheels and remarkably little damaged considering that it had turned over twice on its way down the bank. All the family in the cabin were uninjured but, of the people on the back, there were four dead and thirteen injured. Gordon brought back the wife and children of the driver and as many of the injured as he could get on to the camioneta (our light pick-up truck) with a kind of first-aid man to look after them. One man died as they brought him out to the car; this wasn't really surprising as he was unconscious and they were standing him up, shaking him and shouting at him in an effort to bring him round! What made Gordon sad was that there were three other trucks there just waiting, the owners showing no interest in bringing the injured in to hospital. The aftermath was a considerable headache to the family as, although it was accepted as not the fault of the driver (the road just caved in) the relatives of the dead and injured all claimed damages, some to the extent of demanding money for Roman Catholic Masses for their souls! There is no insurance here, so the unfortunate driver had to cover all costs himself and was not allowed, by the police, to use the truck again till all was paid. Imagine all this for such a new believer. His neighbours all said it had happened because he had been converted. In spite of it all he carried on well, and now the family are inviting their neighbours in to a meeting twice a week.

We are really enjoying our new home and finding it ideal, especially for the work with young people. Two of the owner's six girls come to that meeting. Their own home is horrible and full of plaster images. We pray that they will notice the difference and that our home will always be used for the Lord's glory. Just now we are on a trip, at present in Pacasi. First of all we went to Alcatuyo for a week for Dr. and Mrs. Brown to visit. They wanted to revisit the Christians in the area and 'see how they do.' We had a very happy time together and were all really encouraged at the way some of the folk have stood firm for the Lord in spite of opposition. We had a meeting each night and by the end of the week, thirty were coming. I would think that at least fifty heard the Gospel, some for the first time. It was so good to see these Quechua people crowded together on the benches of that tiny Hall. The school teachers showed quite a bit of interest too. Dr. Brown's Quechua is so very good that it was a good exercise for us too.

Life was not without its lighter moments! The first thing we did on arrival was to install the new water pump we had bought but, oh dear! Much hard pumping failed to produce even a drop of water! Gordon went out to inspect the well and found it had more water in it then ever before. The men folk took the pump down again and tried it in a bucket of water; still not a drop: they poured water in one end but it didn't come out at the other! Eventually investigation showed that the bright mechanic who prepared it for us had put in a solid washer without making a hole through it!

Gordon and I slept on Li-Los which was quite fun and comfy at the beginning of the night but, since both had slow punctures, we found ourselves flat on the floor each morning! On Wednesday we went over to Puna. The road was awful! Gordon was supposed to go over to the Agricultural School but Alfredo couldn't accompany him. I can't take the children at that hour so Roger has the meeting here. The meetings are really good and Roger's Quechua is a joy to listen to. He has been helping us a bit today. Gordon and he talked a lot about language technicalities, which go right over my head, but I showed him my notes of a talk I gave to the women in Quechua and I was gratified to find that there was very little he had to correct.

Raimundo came on a visit from Puna, so Gordon ventured his trip to the Agricultural School and, as has happened before, he got lost in the river bed on the way home, Raimundo having stayed in Puna of course. The road is marked only with the odd stone here and there, and with no moonlight it is easy to lose track. That wasn't all; as he reversed back toward the road he sank into sand up to the back axle. By torchlight he had to dig a hole for the jack, jack the car up, dig under the wheels and then put a path of stones for the wheel to run on to. Three times, the mound of stones gave way and he had to start again, but on the fourth attempt he got away and back on the road. He had only his bare hands to dig with. He should have been home by 9 p.m. At 10 p.m. there was no sign of him. I woke the Browns and we talked and prayed about it and they said if he wasn't back by 11 p.m., Roger would go out and search for him. They went off to sleep again and I waited. I tried to read but I kept running outside to look and listen in the dark night, and running from one window to another. At 11 p.m. I looked out once more before waking the Browns again and there was a light across the pampa. It was Gordon! How thankful I was when he arrived home. I had been really worried. His finger nails are worn right down and are still hurting.

Our preaching expedition to Puna yesterday, Sunday, was good. The crowd listened well in the plaza and a good number turned up for the Breaking of Bread meeting. Our picnic was good fun though, after a morning of brilliant sunshine, it began to rain. All through the meeting it rained and thundered and hailed and we couldn't help giving each other sidelong glances, wondering what the road would be like for the journey home. It was awful! The rain had stopped when we left but we had to wait half an hour or more till the river subsided and we were able to get across safely. There are not many danger spots between Puna and Alcatuyo but we slipped about a lot in the mud and I was happy to be home.

I feel I am too busy these days and my spiritual life is at a pretty low ebb. I can pull myself together and take a meeting fairly effectively, but in my own Quiet Time I find it very hard to concentrate. I find myself thinking about anything except the matter in hand, and my mind wanders in prayer. I know this is a danger signal and feel I shall collapse under the strain of missionary life if I don't live closer to the Lord all the time.

We had a very pleasant, though rather un-missionary interlude on Wednesday. Three British boys called on us and we had a great time with them. They were all in their twenties and absolutely oozing social status, university and adventure! They had such delightful English voices and manners that it was a joy to meet them. One is heading for university in Canada, one on his way home to Surrey, and the other on a world tour with a Land Rover. I think they all plan to write books. They started from the south of the Argentine and are on their way north through Peru, Ecuador, and Mexico etc. up to Canada. They were delightful fellows and we had a lot of fun with them. I felt a bit like Dorothy Warder in La Paz when she met the English cricket team and commented on how nice it was to meet some "good clean English manhood!" They seemed disappointed that they hadn't had more adventures. They have been stuck only once and then they enjoyed hauling themselves out! They should try life in Alcatuyo for a bit!

We are now in Pacasi for a few days and Gordon is having meetings each evening. On Friday morning a mother and her son were baptised. We all went back to the Hall for the usual feast of soup (very peppery), followed by broad beans, potatoes and sweet corn in a pile on the floor. The potatoes are cooked in their skins so you have to peel them with your fingernails (they won't have had much of a wash!) and then dip them in saucer of ají (a very hot sauce of hot peppers ground together with a bit of tomato). This is followed by tea and a dry bread made with ground peanut flour. It was quite fun; we were thankful that their culture meant that we were served first as they had only three or four plates which were passed on from one to another without being washed up in between! Life is never dull!

In April three new missionaries are expected to arrive from England: Mr. and Mrs. Colin Hunns and Mr. Bill Cotton. Please remember them in your prayers.

Uyuni (pg. 27)

Railcar from Uyuni to Potosi (pg. 28)

Pacasi Sunday School with Dr. Hamilton (pg. 51)

Pacasi Mayor and Corporation (pg. 51)

Engagement Photo (pg. 72)

Alcatuyo—Our First Home, Inside (pg. 78)

Preaching in Puna (pg. 86)

Outskirts of Potosi—the "Silver Mountain" (pg. 163)

16
Reinforcements

1963

Suddenly we are quite an English speaking community! I must tell you how it all happened because I know you have been praying. Gordon and I have been so busy here with far more to do than we could adequately cope with, so we were praying that the Lord would send some help. Back in April three new workers came into the country, Colin and Ann Hunns and Bill Cotton, all set to learn Spanish in Sucre. They went first to stay with Dr. Roger and Dell Brown through whom they first heard the call to Bolivia. Soon after they arrived the Browns had to go away, so we invited the newcomers to visit us here in Potosí, and while they were here to take a look around at the opportunities in the work here and in the country places around. We had a great time together. We spent three days in Alcatuyo and from there visited Pacasi. The Christians gave them all a very good welcome and an invitation to stay, and they seemed very impressed with the need and the opportunities.

Our visitors decided to look for accommodation, and if they found it (they had so far been unsuccessful in Sucre) they would accept that as confirmation that they were to stay. In about three days Bill was fixed up with a room in the home of one of the elders of the assembly and Colin and Ann found a very suitable flat. The flat was in the home of a lawyer who offered Spanish lessons in return for English lessons, and this arrangement is working out very well. The lawyer is also a University lecturer and one of Bill's companions is a graduate so I guess they couldn't do much better. They are all well settled in now, accustomed to the altitude, and digging in to Spanish studies, so we are looking forward to their help very soon. They plan to be here for a year while they seek guidance as to where they should ultimately work, so do pray for them about this. We covet their help here. It would be great to have one of them in Potosí and one in the country round about, but there is plenty of need in other parts of Bolivia too.

~~~~~~~~~~~~~~~~~~~~

Gordon and Colin have been away preaching for a few days and Ann came to stay with me. While the men were away the highlight was a party for my Sunday School class. Unfortunately many of the girls were away for the school holidays and only four turned up, but with two other teachers and ourselves we had a lovely time. Ann and I had worked hard preparing attractive food and it went down well. In fact they all took some home with them! It seems to be the custom here to take more on your plate (it is definitely not polite to let a guest empty their plate) than you can possibly eat and take the rest home. We were tickled pink at this undisguised smuggling! (*Later we learned that the hostess is really expected to provide little baskets or boxes for that very purpose!*)

We played the usual party games though they were new to these children and to ours! We played Blind Man's Buff, Hunt the Thimble, Musical Chairs (on cushions) and Musical Parcel. Malcolm and Penny were so excited, especially Malcolm who joined wholeheartedly in the spirit of the moment and laughed and shrieked. He was so happy that he just didn't know what to do with himself. He completely missed the point of some of the games asking, for instance, "Why do we all keep flopping down on cushions?" Penny's greatest joy was blow football and she was ready to do it again first thing next morning. Needless to say we had a bad night after all the excitement, but Malcolm, at any rate, is all set for another party as soon as possible!
~~~~~~~~~~~~~~~~~~~~

~~~~~~~~~~~~~~~~~~~~

Today has been super. We took the Señoritas for a picnic. They had pleaded for one for so long and we weren't very enthusiastic but we felt we had to do it. There were six girls and Ann came too so we were quite a crowd. I provided all the food so that kept me busy. They chose to go to a place called 'Miraflores' where there are hot springs. We didn't know the road at all, but it was only about fifteen miles out of town.

It was super! I've never seen anything like it before. We climbed a little way up the mountainside and there was a series of gorgeous waterfalls and pools amongst the rocks, all with lovely hot water. It was really hot and abundant, and they told us it is boiling a bit further up and you can cook in it! It was really beautiful. We found a little pool for the children and the girls went to a deeper place to bathe. After a picnic lunch we went down to the village where there is a proper little swimming pool, (outdoor) and I had a wonderful swim. It was like being in a hot bath, a rare luxury in Bolivia. The running water came up to my chin when I stood up. The girls enjoyed watching us swim but we couldn't be too energetic because of the altitude. Now we are making plans to go again in September or October, taking the tent, and having a holiday. It is so near to Potosí but quite a bit lower, and we could laze and swim and let the children paddle. We are all quite sunburned today and it is nearly mid-winter!

~~~~~~~~~~~~~~~~~~

Soon after, we had an interesting trip into the country, which I think may be worth recording before the details leave my mind.

A series of fairs animated us into planning a trip around Pacasi and Alcatuyo. We took Colin and Anne, and Bill as they wanted to see what the country work would be like. The pickup truck was piled to the canvas roof, probably overloaded, but the Lord kept us safe on the journey. Preparing for such a trip is about like planning to climb Everest! It involves taking all necessary food, bedding, books for sale, tracts to give away, preaching equipment (loudspeaker, record player, projector, screen etc., etc.) toys for the children and all the other paraphernalia of living! This explains the over loading of the vehicle when you add five adults and two children as well. Unfortunately we had to leave our servant lassie, Lily, behind. There just wasn't room for her.

The journey to Pacasi was uneventful except that we came upon packs of mules on their way to the fair. Each time, we had to stop as the animals tended to panic; they had churned up the road very badly, making it dangerously mushy. Arriving at Pacasi we had our work cut out to get organised before nightfall. It was Wednesday and the next day, was the great day of the fair in Chaquí. Not having Lily created a problem. The girlie who usually helps me in Pacasi has got married since we were here last so she sent along her brother, a boy of fifteen! He was a great help but not exactly practised in the art of civilised washing up, and it was only with difficulty that we persuaded him to change the cold greasy water at intervals. Never mind, we were so busy with other things that he was a real blessing to us, and he was obviously very happy on the job.

We went to Chaquí in the afternoon. There must have been thousands of people there and thousands of mules. We picked our way very carefully to the plaza where, again, mules with drunken or drugged riders where racing round and round the square. Crowds were watching on both sides of the road but the atmosphere was ghastly and, after a quick look at some of the stalls, Ann and I took the children back to the car. I have a very vivid recollection of how Penny nearly went under the hooves of a mule at the fair last year and I didn't want to take any risks. The narrow side streets were especially dangerous as the frenzied animals charged around. We sat in the comparative safety of the car just watching. We heard that several people are killed each year at this particular fair.

The men folk went off to preach where the mules were being sold, but the response was very poor. In spite of the thousands of people there are few who are willing to listen in the midst of such excitement.

Over the same few days there was also a fair in Pacasi where the hearing was better and we managed to sell a good number of books to the men (the women can't read). One evening we took a filmstrip down to the plaza to show there, but we were drummed out. However, quite a crowd followed us back to the house, where we showed the film on the garage doors. Gordon had evening meetings for the believers in Pacasi, and one afternoon I had a women's meeting. This was a bit of an effort and took me ages to prepare as it had to be in Quechua. Only seven women came but as a counter-attraction to the fair that wasn't too bad. I used a flannelgraph on Naaman, an entirely new story to them, but Naaman would keep falling off the board. I kept complaining about him in English until Ann said it sounded as though I was swearing under my breath. I must think of that another time!

On Saturday morning Bill left us to return to Potosí in a shaky old bus as he had other commitments. One of the believers, Valeriana, was on the verge of producing a new babe (she already has two) and it arrived on Saturday. We went to the house but were obviously not welcome nor were we invited in. Mother-in-law was in charge and was not at all friendly. Later, however, she came saying Valeriana was not well and would we go and see her. Ann and I went, (Ann is a nurse too) and we decided that she obviously needed the help of a doctor; meanwhile we gave her Penicillin. The doctor from Puna cycled over next morning and gave his opinion that Valeriana must have an immediate operation and would have to go to the hospital in Potosí straight away. Gordon agreed to make a special trip to take her that afternoon. The doctor left and the old mother-in-law (who had previously lied to cover herself) came to say that Valeriana didn't want to go to hospital. We went to the house and found that troublesome, ignorant, relatives had persuaded her not to go. Her husband is away in Argentina. We reasoned and pleaded, but they said they had no faith in the doctor or hospital and they would 'do it themselves' with the help of the local witch doctor. We had to come away; it was a terrible feeling leaving a Christian girl at the mercy of heathen relatives. Late that night another relative (a believer this time) came pleading for us to take her as they could not do anything. Gordon and Colin took her next morning, making a special journey, while Ann and I packed. By the time the men returned we were ready to reload the car and go on to Alcatuyo.

Unpacking again! Then Gordon went out to put the car away in the garage but the gear had jammed in neutral! Nothing Colin or Gordon could do would move it, so it had to be abandoned outside for the night. The men spent several mornings in or under the car, and in taking the gearbox to pieces, but eventually had to confess themselves beaten. What a timewaster it was! There was nothing else for it but to go to Potosí on any camion (truck) that came by and bring a mechanic back to it.

The camion on which they travelled was piled high with goods but on top were a couple of Cambridge students touring South America. They were grateful to spend the night in our house in Potosí and have a good wash before continuing on their way to Oruro. The mechanic came next day and with Gordon as his 'boy' he got the car fixed in a few hours.

One night, while we were still in Alcatuyo, there was a call at our bedroom window which frightened Gordon and me out of our sleep. It was 4.30 a.m.! An old lady wanted us to go to her daughter who was ill. We were not very enthusiastic, but the lady was a believer whom we knew well and the house was not too far away, so we hauled ourselves out of bed and went. The girl had pneumonia but a heavy dose of sulpha drugs soon put her on the road to recovery.

One day we noticed that our pump water had a suspicious smell, so we had to organise a 'fishing' session! This was a very complicated procedure; to inspect the well we had to get out the car battery, the film projector, a basket, string, and a pole. Two of us worked together, one holding the projector to shine a light on the surface of the water and the other fishing with the basket and line. This session produced some very dead bodies of frogs, rats and mice. We had no disinfectant with us this time so we had to rely on boiling the water for a very long time. We weren't very happy about this and prayed earnestly that the Lord would watch over our health. He did and we are so grateful to Him for it.

Fortunata helped us again in the house. Here is an amazing thing: she actually baths her baby! Usually, even the Indians who work for foreigners and see the way we care for our babies, go back to their old customs when they have babies of their own. Fortunata's baby is a credit to her. She baths him every day, gives him orange juice and puts him to sleep unbound. They usually wrap their babies tightly in cloths like bandages ('swaddling clothes' I guess) to help their limbs grow straight. Incredible! Fortunata has helped me care for Malcolm and Penny and must have learned how to do it, and now her little Demetrio is the bonniest Indian baby of four months that I have seen.

There were big goings-on in Alcatuyo while we were there. August 2nd is the 'Day of the Indian,' and there were several days of festivities. The school was the centre of activities, and the children from thirteen other schools came over to stay, complete with teachers and parents. The fun began with a torchlight procession and the next day there were processions, displays, dancing etc. by the various schools. Later there were football matches and other more adult entertainments. Gordon spent a good bit of time there preaching and Colin proved a tireless salesman of Gospels, Bibles etc. Evening meetings were not well attended because of all the other attractions, and no one came to the women's meeting. Obviously we had to go to them rather than expecting them to come to us on this occasion. It was well worth it though, and the Word of God found its way into many homes through that opportunity. The people were from little villages up in the mountains where they seldom, if ever, hear the Gospel.

We stayed over Sunday and went to Puna to preach in the morning. There was a fairly good hearing though the town was pretty quiet. On Monday we got back to Potosí just in time for the big celebrations here. All the schoolchildren in the town were in procession. There were said to be 5,000 of them and I can well believe it. It pained us to think that of this 5,000, we touch about 50! The others are buried in Roman Catholicism and are taught all sorts of untruths about us…e.g. the Protestants spit on the Virgin. The most impressive thing about the schools here is that each has its own brass band, and some of them put the local military band to shame! They really do put up a good show and there is great rivalry between them.

Now life has settled back into a more normal routine with the usual round of meetings. In September we hope to have a short holiday in Tarija to shake off the influenza that has assailed the children and me, and before the rush of New Year begins.

17
Changes

TARIJA 1963

Well, here we are at last on holiday and feeling lots better already. I have been lazing around and, this morning, had breakfast in bed. My blood pressure is down to almost normal. Our only complaint is that the weather is awful—just about like British holiday weather! Tarija is a very hot place so we brought light summer clothes, and ever since we arrived it has been cloudy and cold.

First though, I must tell you about the journey. We left Potosí at about 10.30 a.m. on Monday. We passed through Alcatuyo first. Colin and Ann had spent the weekend there to sell books at the fair, and we found them sitting fairly cheerfully by the roadside at the school, waiting for a truck to take them home to Potosí. On we went and found quite a nice place for a picnic lunch. Penny slept on Lily's knee in the back of the car and Malcolm had a little child seat between Gordon and me. After lunch we passed over some pretty wiggly steep roads which I don't like a bit. I sit and curl up my toes, grit my teeth and clench my fists just hoping we shan't meet anything on the multitude of blind corners. Then we passed through a very pretty valley of red earth and full of peach trees beginning to blossom. At 5 p.m. we came into Camargo. It was very hot and we shed our woollies straight away. We stayed at a hotel and found it quite reasonable except that there was no light in the bedroom and we had to spend the evening by candlelight.

Our journey on Tuesday was terrific. The hotel in Camargo had been quite good and we got away at about 8 a.m. I was pretty scared for about two thirds of the way as we wound over the mountains, but the scenery was absolutely breathtaking. At about midday we got to the top of the very last mountain and had our lunch. Then we dropped slowly down the 6,000 feet into the Tarija valley. It felt rather the same as coming down to land in a plane for we started above the clouds.

Tarija is a flat city with its streets all at right angles to one another, as they are in most of the towns here. The plaza is very pretty, though so far the weather has been too bad to enjoy it. The buildings are painted in pastel shades and there are enormous palm trees. The house of Mr. and Mrs. Randall is wonderful for the children. First there is a large patio completely paved and with a very big date palm in the centre which shades the patio like a sunshade. Further inside there is another patio with grass and fig trees, another palm tree and then, still further in, a big chicken run which is full of orange, lemon and tangerine trees (and chickens!). When the weather improves it should be a lovely place for a holiday, but I don't think I would like to work here. The town seems awfully quiet after Potosí. It is so nice and peaceful, and now the sun has come out so it is beautifully warm too. To heat the bath water, just stand it outside in the sun and leave till hot! The children are as happy as anything (we brought the bicycle and scooter) in the patio. We are all feeling fine. Gordon was saying this morning that he feels relaxed and able to do things. I feel wonderful except that the cold days at the beginning left me with a cold. We notice how much better we are at this lower altitude. The children are sleeping better too and for several nights we have slept through till after 5 a.m.—quite a record. Hopefully the habit will continue when we get home! At the moment Gordon, Malcolm and Penny are all busy cleaning the car.

~~~~~~~~~~~~~~~~~~~~~~~~
~~~~~~~~~~~~~~~~~~~~~~~~

On the home journey we found quite a good spot for lunch amidst enormous cacti and thorn bushes. This is a very beautiful spot really; much greener than most places and the earth is red. Here we had a puncture, so Gordon and Bill had to change the wheel. It was the dirtiest of places, with thick red sand, and we soon looked like a company of Red Indians! Our shoes were full of sand and later, when I brushed my hair, the brush turned red! It was very hot sitting by the roadside, but it would have been worse in the car. It was about half an hour before we were under way again, and soon we were nearing Camargo. Another slight mishap occurred. We were passing a truck when the driver swung out to the middle of the road and pushed us to one side. The sandy earth gave way and I was afraid the car would tip on its side. It is circumstances like this which make us appreciate the four-wheel drive and extra gears we had on the Land Rover. Never mind. With the Lord's help we were soon unstuck and it wasn't a bit serious. We arrived in Camargo at about 4 p.m. and intended to get ourselves organised in the same hotel and clean before descending on some E.U.S.A. missionaries, Mr. and Mrs. Burns. We felt we were too many to ask for hospitality with them but, on our way into town, Mrs. Burns spotted us, and when she heard we were going to the hotel she just about exploded, "Hotel, my foot! Just you come home with me, we were expecting you." She insisted on putting us all up for the night and had even got a cake ready with 'Malcolm' and 'Penny' on it. The Burns were away when we went through before but their servant lassie had evidently given a good description of us, and we had said that we would be back in two weeks. Their house is very nice with a balcony round a big patio.

Next morning we got away quite early, and the rest of the journey was uneventful. We got home in record time. From then on, things began to go wrong. Our first thought was a cup of tea, as you can imagine, and the pump of the cooking stove refused to function. Gordon spent an hour in vain, trying to fix it. We got our old stove over from the store room and that flooded and went up in flames, so eventually we had to resort to an old Primus stove. We did finally get a rather sad supper and enough warm water to bath the infants, and then the tank ran dry too. Battling with it all, newly back in the high altitude, left us exhausted and bed was never so good. Next day Gordon got both stoves working so we are more or less back to normal.

(I cannot understand why, in this entire visit to Tarija, I have not mentioned the Randalls of New Zealand, Ron and Mavis, who were very dear friends and in whose home we were staying. I can only think that they must have been away and have lent us their home on this occasion. Much later, at the end of our time in Bolivia, they took us into their home for several months and we were so grateful for their hospitality. If this book should fall into Mavis' hands, [Ron is with the Lord] I trust she will forgive me).

~~~~~~~~~~~~~~~~~~~~~~~~~

A Visitor

We have just had such a busy day. I must begin this week's letter while there is opportunity to tell you all about it. I think I mentioned in the last letter that we were expecting a visit from a Bolivian commended worker to have a kind of Gospel campaign. Well, today was the great day of his arrival. We have spent a good bit of the last two days getting beds ready in the room at the back of the meeting hall, where we often slept ourselves. It looked quite posh by the time we had finished. The train was due at midday so the morning promised to be quite a panic. I went out for a minute during the morning and met two very lost American fellows who accosted me and asked in Spanish where they could get some breakfast. After chatting for a few minutes in English, I took pity on them and took them home and set to frying eggs etc. to feed them myself. They were as happy as anything chatting to Gordon, and their breakfast lasted till 11 a.m., while I was hopping from
~~~~~~~~~~~~~~~~~~~~~~~~~

one foot to the other wanting to get on with jobs. They were tourists travelling in a Japanese Jeep – very nice fellows.

Eventually they went and we rushed out to do things in town, checking on the train time…forty minutes late…praise be! That added a complication in that D. Juan, who was to accompany Gordon to meet the guests, would have to be invited to dinner as well! They eventually arrived, plus two children (a boy of nine and a girl of four) and with D. Juan as well, our dinner would only just go round and Lily and I had to go a bit short. We had a bit of a breather while they went to the Hall to organise themselves there, and then Gordon took the brother off to visit one of the elders.

We were five adults and four children. Boy, what a day. I was glad we had arranged for them to sleep at the Hall and get their own breakfast, but we shall be nine for main meals for three weeks. Help! I expect the believers will invite them out to some meals and they are really very easy to entertain, though they are not at all used to our way of living. I am going to be a 'Martha' for the next three weeks, but I don't mind as it is for the Lord. The children, Pascal and Yvonne, will be good playmates for our two.

~~~~~~~~~~~~~~~~~~

Yesterday was a good day. We were thrilled that Sunday School went really well and numbers soared to 114. There seems to be no rhyme or reason in the fluctuations. My class went wonderfully and everything seemed to be good. Then at 6 p.m. we had the first of our new YPF meetings and 30 came, including several strangers. The girls had provided ample refreshments and we all enjoyed the time. This is a new venture to replace the separate boys' and girls' meetings during the week. I think it will go well. We are having it before the Sunday evening meeting (at 8 p.m.) in the hope that some will stay on. It will also save us from the responsibility of taking the girls home. As our special speaker would be preaching, Gordon took our children home to bed while
~~~~~~~~~~~~~~~~~~

I stayed to play the organ for the hymns. Boy, was I tired! I had played for S.S., the YP meeting, singing before the evening service, and then for the service itself!

~~~~~~~~~~~~~~~~~~~~~

We are still in the throes of the campaign and have meetings every night in one hall or another. Gordon and the others are spending their days visiting from house to house and have had some interesting contacts. Of all those who promise to come to a meeting, about one in a hundred keeps that promise. Our visitor is probably the best Bolivian preacher I have heard. He is very good with the children too. So far no one has been saved, as far as we know, and one wonders how they can listen to such forceful messages and go away untouched.

Sometimes folk ask the visiting family out to meals, but they are with us most of the time. We were touched when the assembly treasurer came to offer us a gift to help with all the expense of feeding the family. We really appreciated the kind offer. It is hard work, but the wife helps me quite a bit as we chat. Our house is getting dirtier every day but I'm just not worrying. We'll have a good clean when they have gone. I hope no one else turns up till we are back to normal.

Poor little Penny has been under the weather again and I really thought she was going to have measles. It was a scary time. Her temperature shot up to 103° and she was floppy, even trembley. We got some of our favourite medicine for her and have been watching for spots. Today she is showing real signs of improvement, for which we are truly thankful. Her temperature is down and she is quite lively, even comical! Our visitors came up to say 'goodbye' and she wouldn't speak to any of them, and then in a deep little voice she said, "No puedo hablar." ("I can't talk.") It sent them off in fits of laughter.
~~~~~~~~~~~~~~~~~~~~~

So, they have gone and we are really sorry to see them go. They have been good company and we have enjoyed the chaos of meal-times. The boy, Pascal, didn't like it when they were invited out to eat. He confided to Lily, "I like the gravy, I like lots of it!" Gravy would be new to them. Malcolm has grown up a lot while playing with Pascal, who is ten, and it has been good to see the two boys together. Amongst other things Malcolm has learned to use the scooter properly and is quite proficient. I sent him to the barber the other day and they really cropped him! He looks a proper little Yankee and I can't bear it. We shall have to look for another, less ruthless, barber.

18
Sucre and an Unexpected Outcome

1963

Instead of going to Alcatuyo on Monday as anticipated, we are going to Sucre! There are a number of reasons, and for some time we have been accumulating things to talk over with the Browns. Our visit has come to a head for various reasons. Gordon has business to do there with regard to his driving licence. The one that was stolen over a year ago has never been satisfactorily replaced as the original documents can't be found. We need to talk over various things with Roger and to consult him medically for myself and the children. My blood pressure isn't too good, and other things are bothering me. The only trouble is that we are afraid he will say that I shouldn't stay in this high altitude; we are so happy here it would be heartbreaking to leave. We love Potosí and the people here, especially the Indians, and we really are a part of the assembly and love it. Everything here suits us except the altitude, and we would hate to admit that has beaten us. We have great plans for travelling to neighbouring villages in the next dry season; they are crying out for visits. We can't think of any other part of Bolivia where we would be as happy. We just don't want to budge. There is work here to last a lifetime and we anticipated staying indefinitely. We are asking the Lord will guide us in all suggestions and decisions.

~~~~~~~~~~~~~~~~~~

Here we are, home again. First, about our journeying. The day before we left, Malcolm's temperature went up, but we decided to go all the same. The journey was uneventful except that he was miserable, and from picnic time on, Penny was car sick all over everything! It was desperately hot, and we could hardly stand it, but the car behaved beautifully and we arrived in record time. Coming home was not so good. Everything was fine for the first two hours; then, in a village, a truck was blocking the way so we reversed to let him by, and our gearbox played its usual game and stuck in neutral! We were there for nearly two hours. A local chap came to Gordon's aid, and together they took the gearbox to pieces, put the cogs right, and put it together again. Meanwhile the children and I frizzled in the very hot sun until the man helping suggested we might like to wait in his house. I was so glad of that. I was very sick. Funny, that doesn't happen to me on journeys. Once we got going again all was well. We stopped for tea with the Burrows family in Betanzos and got home at 4.30 p.m.

Malcolm was in bed for most of the time in Sucre and Roger decided it must have been tonsillitis. Gordon had a terrible rash for five days. He must have been allergic to something as he came out all over in large red wheals with blisters. He hasn't had it for two days now, so we hope that incident is over. We have no idea what did it, but the irritation drove him mad. We had a really nice time with the Turners in Sucre. We visited the Browns and we shopped and visited other friends. On Malcolm's only day in circulation he had a great time playing with two future schoolmates. We anticipate that he will go to the B.I.M. school in Cochabamba. We met the Longleys who have Paul (5) and Elisabeth (2), and then the Gales who have Peter (4) and Glenys (1). We took Malcolm's tricycle as he has no chance to use it here and he had a wonderful time. He wanted to stay with his new friends, poor lad.
~~~~~~~~~~~~~~~~~~

Well, I seem to be the biggest problem and we have some big decisions to make. My blood pressure calls for a lower altitude, though it may be due to stress. It does go down when we are at a lower altitude, but I am usually then on holiday and less stressed. What to do about that can be decided later. Meanwhile, I need an operation within the next few months and...well, you remember that sickness on the way home? Tests soon after, revealed that a new baby is on the way! I am shattered. I went back to the chemist for the results; he smiled broadly and said, "Congratulations Señora!"

~~~~~~~~~~~~~~~~~~~~

1964

It is sometimes difficult to see the Lord's hand in adverse circumstances, and yet, in retrospect, we do see dimly what His purpose must have been. It is only in the light of our full salvation that we can understand the Cross.

An operation, the prospect of a new baby, travel difficulties and other problems brought us back to England much sooner than we anticipated. It seemed rather a defeat, it would take such a time away, and yet we were encouraged as the Lord went before us in every detail. We saw His hand as impossible situations were overcome in our planning for the journey and as we travelled the four days by train to Buenos Aires and three weeks by boat from there.

I shall never forget the relief of, at last, meeting with efficient officialdom as we landed at Tilbury and some of our problems were ironed out by some very kindly gentlemen—the baggage agent, a policeman who helped me with the intricacies of dialling from an STD callbox, etc.

Much has happened during these days and weeks at home in the United Kingdom. My mother went suddenly to be with the Lord just five weeks after we arrived. It must have been the Lord's
~~~~~~~~~~~~~~~~~~~~

goodness that brought me back to see her once more and to be with my father during that time. Simon John joined our family—a happy, contented little fellow, who soon endeared himself to us all. Six months later, an operation for me and, in the Lord's goodness I am once again fit and well.

We have been away longer than we anticipated and now the time has come to return to Bolivia. We are going back to Alcatuyo and into the country work again and, being able to visualise to some extent all that lies ahead, we tremble at the prospect. One thing we have learned, and that is that the Lord can do amazing things. Looking back we see that 'Not one thing hath failed of all the good things that the Lord spoke concerning us.' (Joshua 23:14) Looking forward we are confident in the Lord, whose promises are innumerable and cover every possible situation. We seek only His glory and the extension of His Kingdom.

'Faithful is He that calleth you, who also will do it.' (1 Thess.5:24).

19
What More Can I Say?

I find myself literally lost for words! I mentioned in the last chapter that, while we were in the U.K., my lovely mother went to be with the Lord. I had already learned to live without her presence but how I did miss her letters. We returned to Bolivia in July 1965 and I continued to write letters, but not many copies were kept, as far as I know, and I have therefore lost my 'memory material.' In putting this book together, Gordon and I have sometimes said to one another, "Did we really do that?" We did! But we have been amazed at how much we had forgotten. Now we have only our memories with which to fill in those last five years and the style of this book will have to change. May the Lord bring back to our minds anything that could be important.

~~~~~~~~~~~~~~~~~~~~~~~

The journey back was a saga in itself. This time we had **three** children and, as we toiled up from our cabin to a top deck, it always seemed that someone had left something behind, and Gordon was usually the one who had to go down and up again. This time we travelled on a different line across the South Atlantic to Buenos Aires, calling at Vigo (Spain) and Lisbon (Portugal). The ship filled up with Portuguese folk heading for Brazil. We were comfortable and well cared for; we hobnobbed with some of the ship's officers and had the company of a few other missionaries. Most of the Portuguese passengers were not a wonderfully cultured crowd, but we did make friends with a lovely couple from Recife (a Brazilian girl married to an Englishman and with two nice little boys). One day we found ourselves invited to the
~~~~~~~~~~~~~~~~~~~~~~~

Captain's Table to Dinner, and they were there too. We were rather out of our depth, especially when we found ourselves with only water to drink as the Captain announced a toast to the Queen! Oh dear! Very sorry, your Majesty. Just before they left the ship, I had a lovely talk with this young lady and she was keen to hear about the Gospel. She said, "Every night I pray God He show me the truth. I read the Bible and I like." As we sailed into the harbour at Rio de Janeiro, this same couple were standing beside us at the railing waiting to disembark. The girl, whose name I cannot remember, sighed and said, very sadly, "Oh, Brazil, your poor people!" My heart went out to her.

We did have fellowship with the other missionaries on that journey. I had the doubtful privilege of playing the piano for 'Divine Service' on Sundays (you can guess they must have been hard up for a pianist!) and we ran a Sunday School. It is an awful pickle going ashore with 3 young children, but we did visit missionaries in Santos, Brazil and an old friend of Gordon's, Don Barris, in Montevideo.

A highlight of that sea journey was the children's fancy dress parade. We dressed Malcolm and Penny (then aged 5 and 4) as a King and Queen. They looked really good. It is amazing what you can do with towels and crepe paper or card, and the ship's shop was always well supplied with such things.

The train journey from Buenos Aires up into Bolivia took four days in all to cross the Argentine Pampa and then slowly and steadily wind its way up into the Andes Mountains. We had two sleeping compartments with a communicating door to ourselves and, to our joy, it had a separate toilet, a luxury indeed. We had taken a large container of drinking water for use during the four day's journey. It had a tap near the bottom so we stood it on a folding table near the washbasin. Not too long into the journey, yes, you can guess the table gave way and we were paddling in drinking water! We hastily picked up the container and managed, to our relief, to save a fair amount of the water. Then Gordon went in search of an attendant to lend us a mop and bucket to dry up the floor. He came himself, but with a screw driver to fix the table! We mopped up as best we could.

It wasn't a very happy journey as little Simon (now coming up to his first birthday) had a really bad tummy upset and, having used all his disposable nappies on the boat, it was all a bit of a nightmare. I had to wash nappies in the hand basin and hang them out of the train window to dry. The children kept relatively happy with small toys which we 'found' at intervals.

We got quite easily through the customs on the Argentine/ Bolivian frontier, and the train then trundled across to the Bolivian side to go through the whole process again. While waiting I hopped out of the train to send a telegram to say we were on the way and, while I was doing so, the train chugged off up to the station, leaving me to run after it for several hundred yards! It reminded me we were now at a high altitude.

It felt good to be back in Bolivia…the same sights and smells and the familiar sandy desert we have come to look on as home. At last we arrived in Uyuni where we had been invited to stay with Willie and Rae Hill for a short while to re-acclimatise. It was lovely of them to invite us and made a wonderful welcome break in the journey. We arrived at 1 a.m. and were soon warmed and fed and glad to tumble into a proper bed. We enjoyed the Hill family so much and they were wonderful to us but oh, we didn't like Uyuni. How brave they are to stay there! I can't think of anywhere that is dustier, dirtier and colder! The children enjoyed playing with the Hill children, Isobel, Robert and Rachel, but they got very miserable as their skin gradually dried up and cracked and layering cream didn't have much effect. My fingers cracked too and it really hurt. We were able to put up with these things ourselves for we know we are doing it for the Lord's sake, but one of the hardest things is to see the children having to endure it too. They accepted it quite philosophically but we didn't enjoy putting them through it for all that.

We thought everything was going really well but there had to be a hiccough! All our 'In Transit' boxes were meant to travel with us on the same train, but enquiry at the station showed that they had not arrived. They did not turn up on the next train or the next. We began to send telegrams all over the place, but could not locate them. How hard it is to be patient; they did eventually turn up, having been sent on a slow cargo train, and it did prove to be the best thing for customs as they went through quickly in spite of some ghastly stories of overcharging.

Simon didn't get any better and I lost no time in finding a chemist to give advice and sell me something to stop his continual sickness and diarrhoea. He seemed reasonably happy, but no food would stay down. I increased the dose of the medicine. After a day or two Willie very kindly took Gordon to Alcatuyo to get the house ready for our arrival. It was a very long way and they were away for some days while the children and I stayed with Rae. I was worried about Simon; one morning he seemed particularly limp and lifeless in his pushchair and I suddenly realised that his pupils were minute! He was breathing weakly and in short panting breaths and Rae, her Indian helper and I stood round anxiously watching him, expecting him to die at any moment. I went to our room and prayed as only a desperate mother can pray and the Lord heard and answered. I went back and we gave him lots of water and put him outside in the fresh air. Slowly his breathing improved and ours with his. I looked again at the paper from the medicine box and saw that it contained Belladonna. It had probably been poisoning him!

By the time Gordon and Willie arrived back next day, he was very much better though still floppy, and Gordon was horrified. We decided to get on the train that night to Potosí where we knew there was a paediatrician but, strangely enough, he improved vastly on the train and we didn't have to take him to the doctor. The train journey was dreadful. We set out at 3 a.m. with the temperature well below zero. There was no sleeping car and even with blankets and hot water bottles our feet just about stuck to the floor. At Rio Mulato the coach was shunted around for about two hours until dawn gradually broke, the sun came up and we thawed out a little. Next, the altitude problem as the train goes over a pass at 16,000 feet. Arriving in Potosí we were so grateful for a meal with Colin and Ann Hunns and then got installed in the 'Hotel Turista!' The Hunns were ever so kind to us during those days in Potosí, and on Simon's first birthday we set off for Alcatuyo with our baggage and Lily, our servant girl.

Looking back some time later, I realised what I should have thought of at the time, that Simon's problem was probably simply the altitude. I had forgotten that, for our baby, this was his first experience of the Andes and he was no doubt suffering from altitude sickness. Why ever didn't I think of it at the time?

The Lord was good and Simon is now, as I write, proud father of six children of his own!

It was good to be home again in Alcatuyo in spite of the usual problems—the stove didn't work, there were dead frogs in the well, etc. but we soon settled back into the routine of the missionary work and now, for the two older children—SCHOOL!

There were soon signs of blessing. In Uyuni a man had come to know the Lord after two meetings of Gordon's. In Potosí and in Alcatuyo we had a great welcome back. A school teacher whom we have not met before has already been asking for help. He has now heard the Gospel and wants to be saved. We were thrilled because 26 people came to the first meeting, including the school headmaster and seven of the teachers.

Our great need then, was a CAR. We prayed about that.

~~~~~~~~~~~~~~~~~~

Our time in Alcatuyo was short-lived. We moved back to Potosí. Evidently Bill Cotton had gone off to La Paz, an obvious move as he was involved with the organisation of Emmaus Correspondence courses. Colin and Ann Hunns had gone to La Paz for the birth of their second child and planned then to return to the work in Pacasi. I'll quote from a letter written in November 1965.

POTOSI
NOVEMBER 1965

The fun and games of moving house yet again! Having just finished unpacking and settling into a smooth running order, we were packing up again. We camped in the Hunns' vacated flat for a few days while house hunting, and the Lord led us to one which suited our purposes admirably. Gordon nearly went dotty trying to keep out of legal traps and was very grateful for the help of a Christian friend with some legal training. He saved us from many pitfalls. Rents are very high and the best system of getting a decent house is called 'anticresis.' I've mentioned before how you loan a large sum of money for a number of years with the house as security. It is an expensive outlay (goodbye to the car for the moment) but at the end of the time all the money is returned.

Eventually the great day came and we sat on the pile of furniture, awaiting the truck from Potosí. It arrived two hours late and as we loaded up a great audience of Indians sat around to view all our possessions! After a week or two of sweltering hot weather, it began to cloud over and rain, and the driver had omitted to bring a tarpaulin. Gordon went off with the furniture and the rest of us settled down for another night. Next day a missionary friend came for us in his car. We were so grateful for his help. He had a two and a half hour journey to get to us and, what do you think? It snowed and snowed and snowed! Our coats had gone on in the luggage, so we were glad to be inside a car and not on top of a truck. As we
~~~~~~~~~~~~~~~~~~

arrived in Potosí the sun broke through and snow slid off the roofs and went up in steam till it was like a fog! What a climate!

It was hard not to regret leaving Alcatuyo. We seemed to have only just begun and, in the midst of all the problems and disappointments, there were glimmers of hope. The one stumbling block to the Indians is fear of the neighbours and it is holding many back. We were sad to find that some who had professed to trust the Lord had joined with heathen relatives at the feast of 'all Saints,' when the souls of the dead are said to return to earth and need to be presented with food at the graveside. During the feast Gordon and D. Julian Benitez (of Potosí) went to preach in a nearby village. D. Julian is a full time evangelist. He is thinking of visiting Alcatuyo for a week or two at a time now that we have left.

We feel overwhelmed at the moment by all that confronts us, and we are increasingly aware of our own insufficiency. We can only trust the Lord, asking for His strength and wisdom. As we return to the work here in Potosí the following two verses have been in my mind:

2 Corinthians 5:9 *We make it our aim to please Him*
1 Corinthians 14:1 *Make love your aim.*

We really fell in at the deep end! The day after we arrived, Gordon was asked to take the meeting that night, a tall order after moving furniture all day, especially at this altitude. Then, on Sunday, a teacher didn't turn up and I found myself with a class of toddlers with nothing prepared, and I'm scared of little ones! We are hoping not to have Sunday School classes ourselves this time, but to teach the teachers as they really haven't a clue. The older girls are clamouring for a class once more. There is a nucleus of very keen ones and I'm hoping they will bring the lost ones back. We do need wisdom here; it is hard to please the tradition-bound old folk, the go-ahead youngsters, and at the same time do all that is pleasing to the Lord. I want to get a class together for the better class ladies of the town. How hard it is to be 'all things to all women!'

20
Down and Up Again

OCTOBER 1966

Strange happenings don't seem to come our way quite so often these days. We haven't any missionary 'lion stories' to tell and, without a car of our own, we have been confined to the routine life of the town, which seems to produce plenty of headaches but nothing to write home about!

Way back in August we went for a holiday in Montero, in the tropical lowlands of Eastern Bolivia. We all went down to Sucre on the autocarril (an old bus fitted with railway wheels), a six hour journey. After a day in Sucre, Gordon went on by bus to Santa Cruz as he had to be in Montero for meetings. I didn't fancy a 24 hour bus ride with the children, so waited for the plane on Saturday, a short trip of 1½ hours. Gordon expected the weather to get really tropical on this trip so took only light clothes and just about froze in snow! I had a panic in Sucre as, about two hours before the flight, I was told that I must have a permit to take the children (supposedly to prevent kidnapping). This meant finding a certain lady for the official paper, and since she was not in her office we had to chase round to her house. It was a public holiday and she was to be in the official procession soon to start, so we were fortunate to find her.

The weather in Montero was unusually chilly, which suited us very well except that we hadn't taken enough clothes. The McKernons were up to their eyes with visitors, having ourselves, some relatives who arrived unexpectedly from New Zealand. Bill Cotton was staying there for the conference, and they were feeding the 50 or so folks who attended the conference. Into the bargain Shirley was caring for a 6 weeks old Quechua baby whose mother had died in childbirth. It was quite a full house. Gradually the visitors departed, leaving just ourselves and the new baby. We had a lovely time, mainly relaxing, but helping by speaking at meetings and visiting. The weather improved to its usual intense heat and we wilted. The summer must be unbearable. How Noel and Shirley stand it I don't know.

One memory I still have of that holiday time was that of being nearly knocked out by a grapefruit! It was a very windy day and part of the washing line was right under a grapefruit tree. You can guess what happened. As I hung out the washing a heavy grapefruit blew off the tree, hitting my head with a stunning blow! It nearly knocked me off my feet.

The journey back to Sucre was uneventful, and we enjoyed a few days there to re-accustom ourselves to the altitude. On the train crawling back up Gordon had a long conversation about the Gospel with a couple who seemed to be really interested. The worst moment of all was our arrival back in Potosí. I thought all the children would be killed! As we arrived we arranged that Gordon would care for the luggage while I steered the children out on to the platform. Neither of us had bargained for the behaviour of the crowd waiting to board the train for La Paz. Before the train had stopped, a shouting, shoving mob of men with fat Chola women, all with bundles and baskets, were forcing their way in. There wasn't a hope of getting out. I tried to protect the children in front of me and people were shouting, "Careful! There are children here." I was petrified. Then a kindly man took the children from me into his seat and protected them while I battled my way out and then he passed them to me, one by one, through the window! Phew! Thank you, Lord. I don't know how Gordon got out with the luggage.

Our next panic came a few weeks later when a local doctor diagnosed Malcolm as having appendicitis and wanted to operate on him. Too many have died from such a simple operation here so we decided to seek more reliable help in La Paz. I took Malcolm and Simon to La Paz and Gordon stayed at home with Penny. We arranged to go on a coche-motor, a rather splendid one-coach train on which meals are served and which boasts a toilet. The journey takes 13 hours. We were due to leave at 11 a.m. and arrive in La Paz at midnight. Unfortunately the coche-motor arrived from Sucre with a broken spring and it was decided unsafe to send it on. We were eventually sent off in the autocarril to Rio Mulato (5 hours) where another coche-motor would meet us and take us the rest of the way. There were two autocarriles. I was in the first one and the poor thing wasn't strong enough to get up the gradient and had to be nosed gently up by the one behind. There was no toilet on this one and it didn't stop long enough to hop out! Malcolm was very good but Simon was impossible. He insisted on standing up on my lap and reduced my thighs to mincemeat! People around us gave the children all manner of things to eat—biscuits, cake, dirty old Indian breads, sweets etc. Then a man borrowed our plastic mug to give them some papaya juice and afterwards used the mug himself and passed it to his wife! We arrived at Rio Mulato: no coche-motor. The men all got out and just about bullied the station master into sending us on till we met it. (I hopped out to the station toilet, a hole in the ground so dirty it doesn't bear thinking about). We pressed on and eventually met up with the coche-motor in Oruro four hours later. Oh the bliss of getting into a clean coach with tip back seats. The children slept at last. The last half hour of the trip is marvellous as you enter La Paz. We slid down the mountainside into a fairyland of lights below. I had forgotten how beautiful it is. We arrived at 4 a.m. I was fortunate to get one of the few taxis to the Warder's house and pile into bed.

After all that Malcolm, didn't have appendicitis! We went to the American Clinic who assured us he didn't have any such thing. He had something much more easily dealt with—worms!

We spent a luxurious day or two in La Paz, and our journey home was uneventful except for the irrepressible Simon.

SNIPPETS FROM OTHER LETTERS OF 1966

The women's meeting has been plodding faithfully along, and the ladies who take part are very, very faithful but, oh so doleful. I have really wanted to help them but they rarely ask me to speak; it is difficult to know how to be tactful about it. One day I got them to collaborate with me by asking their help in a special campaign for women in one of the Quechua halls. I think they felt it was a worthy idea but not very likely to work! I told them I would like to do the series of talks myself to practise my Quechua. It worked well. Alas, no one professed to be saved, but the believers caught the enthusiasm and gradually began to bring others. We doubled our numbers from 18 on the first day to 36 on the last, plus the usual crowd of unruly children. We did all we could think of to attract folk in with hymn singing over the loudspeaker, posters and invitations, and we are now hoping to repeat it in another area.

While I was busy with the women, Gordon took some lads out distributing leaflets with informal meetings here and there. The two boys are aged 15 and, though they are simple lads, in the short time they have been saved they show far more promise as believers than any of the others. They are far more helpful than any of the University types whose zeal is all talk! We pray that they will not be spoiled but will remain firm in their testimony.

The latest addition to our family is a new car! It is a Toyota 'Jeep' which we bought from Colin and Anne when they left for furlough three weeks ago. It is small for our family needs, but good for negotiating Potosí's steep, narrow, cobbled streets. We shall have to get a trailer to carry camping gear when we go out into the country, but it has already proved useful for carrying water from a distance in the present shortage. On one occasion, before they went away, Colin helped us by carrying water from Lily's house. He and Gordon took a 66 gallon drum in the car and filled it with buckets of water. Of course it was terribly heavy and they crept home. As the car jolted, poor Colin, who was driving, got about a bucketful of water down his back and had to change completely into some of Gordon's clothes. He won't forget that good deed in a hurry! On another occasion a loving Christian lady brought us a bucket of water from her well, walking with it from the other side of town. What wonderful love!

MARCH 1967

The next thing that happened was that the Browns offered us their little caravan. We thought we couldn't afford it but the Lord sent along some cheques that exactly covered the cost, so we set off in high spirits to Sucre to collect it. It was a good journey and we camped for one night in a river bed on the way home to try out our new travelling home. We hadn't taken the Igloo tent with us so had to squeeze in. The children and I slept crosswise in the caravan and Gordon in the back of the Toyota. I have never had such an uncomfortable night. I thought I would be OK curled up, but spent a good bit of the night with my legs up the wall! Anyway, with the Igloo tent there will be plenty of room for all.

Our first real journey was to Pacasi, a mere thirty odd miles away, to have meetings with the believers over Carnival; easy, one would think! However, the road was dreadful and we bounced along, fearful of the springs. The caravan followed patiently, but both Toyota and caravan suffered badly. A tyre of the car was split, ruined in fact, and some rivets on the caravan had broken. This was originally a front wheel assembly and the steering had been fixed but it had come adrift and the wheels were crazily free once more. Fortunately a Christian in Pacasi with considerable brawn and a fair bit of brain was able to help Gordon to get it temporarily repaired for the journey home.

We enjoyed those days in Pacasi. Again, there were about 20 adults and a crowd of children who stayed for dinner between meetings. I made an enormous pot of soup each day and the womenfolk brought beans and potatoes which were piled on a mat in the middle of the floor. The children thought it tremendous fun to peel the cooked potatoes with their finger nails. For tea we had coffee and Indian bread which, while tasting like sawdust, isn't too bad dipped in the coffee. Malcolm and Penny enjoyed helping to prepare the vegetables in the evenings, and Malcolm became a real adept at grating carrots. We found a lovely stream in which the children were able to bathe a couple of times and, since the scenery is gorgeous, we decided that missionary life is not so bad after all! All went well on the journey home except that the silencer came adrift; Gordon spent half an hour on his back in deep mud as it was raining hard.

21
High Altitude—High Society

AUGUST 1967

We have new adventures to write about - but something right out of our depth. We have been hobnobbing with high society!

It all began on Tuesday evening as the ladies from my meeting were just leaving; a message filtered through to us that His Excellency the British Ambassador was here in Potosí and was looking for us. Next morning Gordon went off to the one posh hotel in town, but he was not staying there. The receptionist suggested that we should go to the 'Prefectura' as she had heard on the radio that he was there on an official visit. The 'Prefect' is the top-notch man in the city, above the Mayor. At last Gordon found the Ambassador and his wife and several other important people, only to learn, to his dismay, that we were expected at a cocktail party that same evening! As you can imagine, cocktail parties just don't come into our way of thinking, but we decided that, as the Ambassador represents the Queen, we had better obey the Royal Command. We expected to be lost in the crowd anyway. I was scared stiff.

In typical Bolivian fashion the invitation was bungled; it said 5 p.m. but was meant for 7 p.m. so, all dressed in our Sunday best we had to go home again! A couple of hours later we mustered our courage once more. I was very shy of addressing the Ambassador as 'Your Excellency.'

We found ourselves among about twenty guests: the Prefect, the Mayor, the Colonel of the Regiment, other military officers and the wives of all. I was the youngest there. We are the only British folk in Potosí, hence the honour no doubt. We managed to avoid the alcohol without too much comment and, while Gordon joined the men, (having a difficult time as they started telling dubious stories) I found myself beside the Ambassador's wife. She was so charming that I find it hard to describe her, and so completely and utterly English. They have been in Bolivia only six weeks and she speaks very little Spanish so she was very pleased to see me. We had a long chat and I found myself as interpreter between her and the Prefect's wife. There were speeches and toasts to the President, the Queen etc., and then we left, but only after the Ambassador had whispered an invitation into Gordon's ear. They were staying in a special railway coach with sitting room, bedroom, kitchen etc. so we were invited to visit them there, at the station next evening at 8 p.m. Meanwhile their day was full of official visits to the mines and other places of interest, plus a broadcast or two.

When we arrived at the Reservado, as the railway coach is called, we were somewhat appalled to find it full with the Prefect, the Colonel etc. and the wife of one of them. The Ambassador's family were there, a boy of 18 on holiday from Eton and a girl of 13, also from a prestigious school, and a lovely little dog. How nice it was to see a clean English spaniel! The poor little thing was suffering from the altitude and was sick! Nigel, the boy, played his guitar and sang, though not very willing until his father whispered in his ear, "Duty!" He seemed a very musical boy, though it wasn't altogether my style of music. We were left as the only guests and we had a really nice evening. They had in the past used the PNEU Correspondence Course for their daughter and found it very satisfactory, so we had a good basis for conversation. They were borne off on the train to La Paz during the night.

Maybe all this doesn't sound very missionary, but you see we had prayed for a point of contact with the well-to-do people of the town who are untouched by the Gospel. Now we are at least on nodding terms with some of them, and that may make us more acceptable to others.

The Ambassador's wife (or perhaps I should put 'Her Excellency,' I don't really know) said to me, "You know, we have much in common in our work, for we have a Mission and you have yours." I agreed that this was so and said, 'You represent the Queen and we represent our King,' and quoted '...now then we are ambassadors for Christ...' We are, aren't we, if we are His? Seeing the dignity with which the Ambassador and his wife carried themselves made me wonder whether we always '...walk worthy of the calling wherewith we are called.'

22
The Downward Trend

SEPTEMBER 1968

Last weekend we were really encouraged as three people from one family were saved; the father and mother on Saturday night and the eldest daughter on Sunday.

The children are all spotty with chicken pox! A national worker and his wife came here for a week of meetings, bringing his wife and little boy, and (as we later discovered) chicken pox. We probably took it to Sucre as we went straight there for a two week holiday and our kiddies had a wonderful time playing with the Turner grandchildren. At the end of the holiday Penny began to feel ill. She and Simon succumbed as soon as we got home, and now Malcolm is in bed all spotty too.

We are very busy. The Bissets are moving yet again. I have to confess that the high altitude of Potosí has beaten me at last and Gordon is also feeling under-the-weather now. It is too much to put all the details here of how the Lord has led us. Briefly, the lease on this house finishes at the end of October so we have to move somewhere. We felt the choice was between three possibilities... another home in Potosí, or in Sucre or Tupiza. The altitude precludes the first, the second 'door' closed but the third opened wide, so we are going ahead and plan to move to Tupiza at the end of October, confident that it is the Lord's will. We had a very encouraging welcome from the believers in Tupiza and the hearty approval of fellow workers. The believers here kindly don't want us to go and panic about what will happen but they are quite capable of carrying on, with the Lord's help. The two Quechua assemblies are no problem, they go from strength to strength, but the Spanish assembly is weak and needs our prayers. Inevitably some of the half-hearted and worldly folk will go, but a nucleus will carry on with the Lord's help, and win others. Tupiza is at 10,000 feet, but it should be a considerable relief from the 14,000 feet of Potosí.

Student riots continue here with the accompanying gas bombs etc. Various friends have warned Gordon not to go out in case he should be taken hostage. Gas bombs are horrible! One was exploded right by the Hall and, although it was well aired during the week, the following Sunday we felt our tongues swelling up uncomfortably. The night it happened, poor old D. Marcial, who serves the Lord as a kind of caretaker, came to our house and told us not to go to the Hall because of the gas. The poor man's speech was almost unintelligible because his tongue was so swollen. Tears are one thing but the eyes sting terribly as well.

TUPIZA, CHRISTMAS 1968

(Written by Gordon this time)

Yes, Tupiza, not Potosí! How green, colourful and restful this valley seems after the stern beauty of the high country around the old mining city. Here, to the East and West of the sleepy little town, steep crags of terra-cotta red provide a contrast of ever-changing beauty behind the green of willows and pepper trees; they seem also to wall in the breathless noonday heat. How strange it feels to be hot! We suspect that, later on, winter frosts will summon back the pullovers and coats, but just now short-sleeved shirts and summer dresses are comfortable from dawn till dusk, and midday temperatures have read over 90°F on the dining room thermometer.

We are back to the home where I was kindly received by Bert and Eileen Randall in my single days, my first year in Bolivia. The rooms are upstairs, over the meeting hall. Built of wood and sheet iron, with inside panelling of three-ply, it feels rather like an oven, even with doors and windows open, but it is an interesting change after the chill of Potosí, and we love the views all around. This front room, our sitting room cum study, is relatively cool, being sheltered by a fine weeping willow tree. On a previous visit, of which I wrote several years ago, we used it as a bedroom but found it too noisy because of activity in the street below and in the railway station beyond.

The church here gave us a warm welcome. They do not really need missionary help, having carried on well for some years with only occasional help from national workers. When the present rainy season has passed we hope, God willing, to visit some of the country places around. At the same time there is plenty of scope for work amongst the children and young people and amongst the women. It is a delicate task to suggest improvements without ousting the older brethren from their rightful place of leadership. The women's meeting has revived with Betty's presence and ministry, and we have just recommenced the Young People's group and hope also to get the Sunday School into classes. At present it comprises all ages from nine months to ninety years! There are one or two brethren who are gifted to preach in the open air, and the use of our loud speaker has encouraged them to start this witness again. Interest seems good.

We are disappointed that, after all, Betty continues to have heart pains, although other symptoms of high blood pressure have abated. Treatment by a local doctor seems to be effective and we are praying that the Lord will give health and strength to complete this year which we believe to be His will for us. The children love it here and, now that they have finished their exams, they will probably be keener than ever for picnics along the valley.

The end of the year has come and we praise God for His faithfulness in the Gospel for we have seen folk saved. We thank Him for providing for our needs. We thank him for fellow believers at home, too, who have worked together with us by prayer and we trust will continue to fellowship with us in this way through the New Year. We long to be really effective for the Lord during what we expect to be our last twelve months in Bolivia.

TUPIZA, APRIL 1969

Part I—Gordon's bit.

I have just returned from a country conference at Cheque, a tiny village about 15 miles down the valley from Cotagaita. Bert Randall and I went with a national worker and a crowd of young people who had come with him. To our great relief we found that the road down the river bed was useable. Getting no certain information about this, we had taken the minimum of baggage in case we had to walk all the way from Cotagaita or hire animals there. This latter prospect horrified me as I cannot ride! The Cotagaita believers had animals ready for us, but one of them threw the man who attempted to mount it, so one can imagine my plight had I attempted to steer such a mount across the numberless fords down river.

Someone calculated that there were 250 people at the conference and, although I suspect that number must have included infants and dogs, there was a big crowd, and the Indian sisters worked like Trojans to cook two half oil-drums of food for each meal besides gallons of 'palque' coffee for breakfast and 'tea.' Palque is a coffee-like drink made from the beans of a wild plant. It tastes vaguely like coffee and is sometimes quite nice.

Once the conference started, meetings went on all day and evening, the three visiting missionaries speaking by turns. In between meetings and meals, we sang. I have never known such a conference for singing! Some would start up at 4 a.m. (alas!) and some would carry on after the last meeting until midnight (alas again!). The odd thing was that the heartiest singers seemed to be tone deaf. We attempted to steer them through the tune but, even after singing it twenty times, as soon as we stopped, they at once got miles off the tune and timing. Some tunes had passed through so many revised versions since being taught at last year's conference that they were unrecognisable. One just hopes that their theology does not get as muddled! The rapid indigenous growth of the scattered churches in that area imposes a strain on the men gifted to teach.

Part II—Betty's bit.

My part of this account is inevitably more domestic. We have had several visitors lately. Mr. and Mrs. Parish came who once worked in Bolivia but have been for some years now in Jujuy, Argentina. We had meetings every night while they were with us, and we ourselves much enjoyed the refreshing of talking to other missionaries. It boosts one's morale to have a good old natter with someone who understands the problems and has some of their own. Then Bert and Eileen arrived back from New Zealand, after five and seven years away respectively. Their children are now grown up so they are free to be back in the work again. While Bert and Gordon were off on the trip described above, Eileen and I have enjoyed some very happy times together.

A boy who has been attending for some time came to the Lord on the eve of his departure to La Paz for military service (2 years compulsory here). The army is a tough place to begin one's Christian life. Please pray for him. Another unlikely lad slouched in one day; we have seen him several times before and always felt he looked a bit like a 'mod' or a 'rocker' (I don't know the difference!). I talked to him at the door (you don't ask men in if your husband is away) and found he had been saved two months ago in the border town of La Quiaca. He had been in some little village, evidently witnessing for the Lord as he said there were several interested folk there, and he said he had given away his Bible and hymnbook and please could he buy a new one as he missed them. He came to the prayer meeting and prayed so clearly that we felt he had really come a long way in two months.

Plans for our journey to New Zealand are not getting along very fast but, so far, we have provisionally booked to travel on the 'Aranda' (Shaw Savill Line), leaving Panama on 26th November and arriving in Auckland on 21st December, just in time for Christmas. It will be Gordon's first visit to New Zealand since he left in 1953.

~~~~~~~~~~~~~~~~~~~~~~

TUPIZA, JULY 1969

In everything that happens to us we see the Lord's hand over us, and in future plans please read a very large GOD WILLING over it all. We make our plans prayerfully and then look to Him to open up the way.

A few weeks back we had a horrible scare with Penny. Symptoms seemed to indicate a rheumatic heart condition. She had three weeks in bed and another doctor confirmed the diagnosis. Both suggested an electrocardiogram in Cochabamba. We took her there and coincided with the conference of missionaries there. It was a horrible journey but we had a wonderful time. It was so refreshing to sing hymns in English again! The cardiologist pronounced Penny perfectly fit and her symptoms insignificant, which leaves us wondering whether the diagnosis was incorrect or whether the treatment and much prayer healed her at the beginning of trouble. We praise the Lord for the outcome. The same cardiologist said that, while Penny was fine, I myself am the problem. My blood pressure was higher than it has ever been. He advocated 1) get out of the high altitude as soon as possible, 2) a pill every day till I leave Bolivia, 3) no added salt, 4) no work!
~~~~~~~~~~~~~~~~~~~~~~

Because of this we have decided to move further down, to Tarija, which, at 6,000' is considerably lower than Tupiza. Ron and Mavis Randall have repeatedly invited us there and Gordon will be able to care for the assembly while Ron goes off on country trips. We shall share their home but I have insisted that we live independently as I feel that five Bissets as guests for five months is too awful a thing to do to anybody! We are selling up nearly all we have so that there will be little to move, and we shall be living with borrowed things until we go.

So we got home from Cochabamba to start packing; 'no work' for me! Chaos reigned! In the midst of it all we had a funeral, and then a young woman from Potosí arrived to collect some things we had promised her. She had a long miserable train journey and then, in the dark (and wearing dark glasses!), she took a header down the back stairs on to concrete and we feared she had fractured her skull. I was frightened. She had the symptoms of a fractured skull and the doctor feared so too. No x-rays on Sunday so we waited and prayed. On Monday she was a little better and we began to hope it was just severe concussion. Today is Wednesday and she is very much more like herself, and we do thank the Lord that all is well and that we can relax a little. It has been an anxious few days. In the midst of all this I had to speak at the women's meeting and Penny got a fishbone stuck in her throat! It was about an inch long and I managed to get it out with a pair of forceps from my chiropody instruments, but it was a nasty few moments. So, as Gordon says, "Never a dull moment." Oh, and I nearly forgot, poor little Simon had a birthday and is now five years old. Apart from presents and a cake, it wasn't a very exciting day for him but we'll give him a treat when things calm down a bit. That brings us up to now. Now for the future.

As mentioned before we are booked to arrive (by boat) in Auckland on 21st December. At the end of July 1970, we set sail again, this time on Chandris Line 'Australis' via Panama, arriving in England on 25th August. This gives us time to pack the children off to school in September, Malcolm to Scarisbrick Hall and Penny to Clarendon. It depends, though, on whether the Local Education Authority will be willing to give us a grant. They have done so for others and we pray it will be the same for us.

23
Down Again and Out

PANAMA
24th NOVEMBER 1969

The Bissets join the 'Jet Set' (third class)! It was, I suppose, great fun flying from Cochabamba to Panama City, but the stops in between left us feeling like the man who travelled from Jerusalem to Jericho and fell among thieves who 'stripped him, wounded him, and departed leaving him half dead!'

Stage I: We left Cochabamba mid-afternoon on Saturday feeling very keenly that this would be our last day in Bolivia. We had already sadly said 'goodbye' to the Randalls in Tarija and now it was to the McKernons, our best pals, and others. The flight to La Paz took an hour, and we then had five hours to wait. La Paz airport (13,000') was cloudy and therefore cold with snow on the mountains around, so we piled on the woollies and crouched over a stove. It wasn't easy to entertain the children, especially as bedtime passed, but the time flew more rapidly than we expected and, after the inevitable formalities, we were on the jet that would take us to Lima, Peru.

Stage II was a Boeing 707 which looked big from the outside and positively enormous from the inside—six seats in a row and thirty rows. We enjoyed the smooth flight, and in one hour and twenty minutes we were landing in Lima. The lights of Lima, seen from the air, were absolutely marvellous. Phew! The heat was terrific in contrast to La Paz, and it was in Lima that we really had trouble. We had to transfer ourselves and our baggage from Braniff to Apsa airlines in a very short time, and we got totally lost in the vastness of that international airport. We felt like country cousins. Gordon, being very short-sighted, found he could not read the signs; neither of us could hear as our ears were blocked from the change in pressure, and the children were dead tired and trailing along in a weary little band behind us. The walls were all of glass, and we had the frightening feeling of being lost in a maze or like a fly on a window pane, and the notice we wanted was always on the other side! Reflections were confusing too; once Gordon called to my reflection when I was walking towards him anyway. Horrible! And everyone we asked was too busy with their own affairs to help much until, at last, a kindly employee to whom I explained our problem said, scratching his head, "Well, what do we do about that?" The problem proved to be that we had come off into the transit lounge instead of right out and back again as we were changing airlines. In the end our kind man found an Apsa employee who led us to the right place, and all was well. It added to our panic that we thought we had only one hour for this and time sped but, huge relief, Lima was an hour behind La Paz so we had 11 p.m. to midnight twice!

Stage 3: Another jet, not quite as large, but still with well over 100 passengers. The children dozed fitfully and we arrived in Panama at about 3:30 a.m. Again the lights were like fairyland from the air. We got through the immigration formalities and out to a taxi. The customs officers made us open every one of our cases, though they didn't find anything to charge us for, and the final straw was that the porter who moved our cases on a trolley about 10 yards charged exorbitantly. The taxi driver was kind and chatty on the half hour ride into the city and didn't charge extra for our white faces. We were horrified to see the number of people, including children, who were sleeping rough on the streets. What a relief to fall into bed in a cool room at last. The discovery next day of several Gideon New Testaments in the Hotel lounge made it really feel like home.

Panama is very hot and humid but we are enjoying it. It is a beautiful city and shopping is good so we have been able to buy some suitable clothes for the ship. Tomorrow the ship arrives from London and we go on board to settle in for three weeks. Next report from New Zealand, God willing.

AUCKLAND, NEW ZEALAND
FEBRUARY 1970

How quickly time flies; one month has passed already of our seven months in New Zealand. I am loving it here, and this morning a wave of temptation swept over me as I thought how nice it would be to settle down in a home of our own, with Gordon in a job and the children in school, and to stay here. I felt almost guilty of treason after such thoughts, and I wouldn't really change my lot of doing the Lord's will, not even for all the pleasures of New Zealand. I suppose all this began because yesterday all three children started school, and we celebrated this extraordinary new found freedom by having coffee in a beautiful tea room on Mount Eden which overshadows the house which has been lent to us. The view is superb and gives a sense of spaciousness. There are no tenements in this city! Each house has a garden all round and there are few tall buildings.

School for two days has been quite an experience for the children. It is a school which gives demonstration lessons to trainee teachers, so the staff are very competent. It is a small world. Malcolm's teacher was born in Bexhill (as I was too, and it is my father's home now); Penny's teacher says he knew her daddy before he went to Bolivia, though we haven't yet discovered who he is, and the headmaster's secretary has been in Buenos Aires and spoke to the children in Spanish. We pray that this experience of school will prepare the family for the bigger experience of boarding school when we arrive in England. They are still rather timid about the big wide world. Perhaps Simon tends in the other direction; he is completely uninhibited!

The Christian folk here have given us a wonderful welcome, even though we missed our official 'Welcome Home.' The boat took us first to Sydney (we waved to the shores of New Zealand) and then back to Auckland. Unfortunately a strike by tug workers kept us in Sydney for three days and, by the time we got to Auckland, most people had gone away for their Christmas holidays! I guess it was good to see something of Sydney, but it was very frustrating!

We have been lent a lovely little house. Washing up is a joy! We have water on tap, no buckets and bowls, not even a Primus stove to boil the water! We have now been lent a little Volkswagen car and Gordon had to do a driving test as his licence is not valid here. He sailed through the written, oral and practical tests, but nearly got thrown out on eyesight. They gave him his license but he finds night driving impossible. I hope to get on to a bit of practice as I didn't drive in Bolivia. I haven't a shred of confidence but I must do it as Gordon will be away quite a bit and one of us must be able to drive at night. In April Gordon is going to the South Island, to the Christchurch and Nelson (his old home) area to take meetings for about three weeks. In the May holiday we hope to all go to Hamilton to visit some tourist attractions as well as take meetings. Later in the year Gordon hopes to go on to Wellington and Palmerston North. I would like to go too but I expect I shall have to stay with the children. Meanwhile the thirty or so assemblies in the Auckland area are keeping us busy.

We really have enjoyed the holiday, going out and about to some of the lovely beaches around. We have also enjoyed time with Gordon's sister, Jean and family. Her husband, Rev. David Aiken who, having been for many years a C.M.S. missionary in

Pakistan is Deputy Director of the New Zealand Bible Training Institute and the family live on campus.

There is no particular news to report from Bolivia at present. I find it hard to believe that I shan't one day wake up and find myself there.

~~~~~~~~~~~~~~~~~~~~~~~~~~

We have never been back to Bolivia but our hearts are there and we pray for the work there every day. The problem was, where next? We had often talked of possibilities, considering Spanish-speaking countries with a lower altitude such as Argentina or one of the other South American countries. There were also the Lowlands of Eastern Bolivia, the Orient. There were other considerations though: our aging parents in the UK and the education of our children loomed large in our thinking.

One day we came upon the verse in Ezra 7:18, [in the King James Version] "Whatsoever shall seem good to thee, and to thy brethren …that do after the will of your God." The Lord spoke to us through this verse. We had often thought that to serve the Lord in Spain would be an obvious thing for us to do and it appealed to us. From there we would be within easy reach of our parents and of the children in boarding school. Accordingly we decided to ask our 'brethren' what they felt about it. We each wrote to the churches which had commended us to Bolivia. We wrote, too, to 'Echoes of Service' in the UK and to 'New Zealand Missionary Funds,' [now 'Global Communications'] and from all these we had an enthusiastic reply. We also wrote to Mr. Ernest Trenchard of Madrid, now with the Lord, a leader of the work in Spain. He replied, saying wisely, "Come to see and be seen."

We attended the Annual Conference in Madrid in October 1970, praying that the Lord would show us His will. We were very warmly welcomed there. In May, 1971, we moved to León in Northern Spain at the invitation of the church, and much later on to Ares in Galicia, until September 1997 when we retired back to the UK.
~~~~~~~~~~~~~~~~~~~~~~~~~~

Appendices

Thoughts on Education Missionary Kids

The picture is engraved on my mind! Imagine a very large patio of uneven grey paving stones and with similar stones built up as a seat most of the way round. Rooms take up three sides of the area, and on one long side is a double wooden door leading to the outside world. In a corner is some kind of pine tree giving shade from the bright sunshine, and under that tree a low square wooden table with kiddie-size chairs round it. School is in progress; Malcolm and Penny are working seriously and the irrepressible pre-school Simon is determined to climb over the table. Read on to see how we coped!

What a joy it is to see our missionary kids grow, and grow up; and yet as time goes on there is a nagging fear in the back of the parents' mind that one day separation from them is going to be inevitable. It is part of the sacrifice missionaries are called upon to make, but the repercussions in the family are enormous. We, ourselves, have been called by the Lord to serve Him and have, in adulthood, left our parents. This may have been costly, to them, as well as to us, but we have all, with the Lord's help, been able to cope. After all, it is normal for a couple to set up their own home, and many other callings, professions, jobs, or just plain fancies can take them to the other side of the world. Nowadays, the world has 'shrunk' with fast travel, telephones, mobiles, and email so that communication is instantaneous and thereby any separation is mitigated to some extent. For us though, in South America, it meant three weeks by boat and then three or four days by train: we could not possibly afford to fly. It took three weeks for letters to arrive (even by air) and another three weeks for the answer to get back. There were, indeed, telegrams which were quite fast, and inland calls could be made over the radio, though they crackled and had to be brief, but neither of these were very satisfactory. We just couldn't leave such little children in the homeland, even though some brave souls of the past did so, and didn't see their children again for five years or more!

What then, is the missionary to do with his children? They must be properly educated in common with their peers, but it is our responsibility to bring them up in 'the nurture and admonition of the Lord' as the Authorised Version of the Bible says (Ephesians 6:4). We were in Bolivia having made that choice for the Lord's sake, but our children had no choice in the matter. I mentioned in a previous chapter how it hurt us to see them suffering cold, chapped cheeks, hands, and sore lips (though this was counter balanced as we moved lower into warmer climes where, climate wise, life became idyllic).

The fact remained, though, that these children whom the Lord had given to us were going to face the future as unusual children and would perhaps become unusual adults. There are various options open in these circumstances, and here all missionaries differ and have to prayerfully balance circumstances, leading from the Lord, and the character of their children, and then do as their own hearts and consciences deem best.

Local schools in Bolivia were just not an option. In the towns it might have been possible, but the system of learning was to get everything off parrot fashion and reproduce it for the exams. Understanding was not involved. (Please remember that I write of Bolivia in the past and things may have changed). We noted this amongst the Sunday School children; they could learn the whole of John's Gospel and repeat it word for word, but they could not tell you, in their own words, what a verse meant. I should, in fairness, record that one missionary couple whom we knew did send their family to local schools, (they lived in the capital city) and it evidently worked well in their case as, I think, all of them became professionals).

There were two schools for missionaries' children in Bolivia, and we assumed that our children would go to one or other of these eventually. Both were American. Children started there at five or six years old and we just couldn't bear the thought of parting with them at such an early age. New Zealand friends were doing correspondence courses with their families and this seemed an excellent idea. We wondered if there might be one from Britain and began to make enquiries. I cannot remember how we found out about them; it may have been through the Warders who moved in the British Community (mainly diplomats) in La Paz. We were introduced to the P.N.E.U. (now called P.U.S., 'Parents Union School,' the correspondence section of the P.N.E.U.) This served us very well indeed for something like 9 or 10 years.

The P.N.E.U. school was not an easy course for parents! The courses we had seen from other countries made life easy with work books and printed sheets. We were sent the text books with the term's requirements as 'Term I Chapters 4 to 8' or 'pages 45 to 100,' and it was left to the parent to get that much information into the child in the term. We had to be serious and I dedicated every morning to 'School.' There were no complaints. The children accepted it philosophically as part of life. The P.N.E.U. system was 'narration,' a single reading, requiring total concentration, and the child was then expected to tell it back. It worked well, and when they did finally take up school in the U.K., they were well up to standard for their age.

While I was with the children, Gordon was able to study. I could not have done this without help with the general housekeeping chores but, in the high altitude and with life very primitive, I needed this help anyway. After lunch Gordon would then take them for a nature walk or do the handwork lessons (not my line!) while I had a rest. We would then leave the children in the care of the servant girl and go visiting, though sometimes we would take them, too. When we went on trips, 'School' went with us. We had then to do a bit of 'flexi-time' but we tried to be disciplined in the amount of time we spent on lessons. I enjoyed it and learned a lot myself! Malcolm and Penny did school together, there being only a year between them. Simon, the toddler, loved to climb over the table and became such a nuisance that we had to pay a girl to take him out and keep him entertained! After supper we had a reading time together and read aloud the children's classics: Alice in Wonderland, Peter Rabbit, King Arthur and his Knights, Robin Hood etc. Our 'Granny Bisset' (who had moved to the UK some years previously to live with her daughter – Gordon's twin) had given us a whole series of these when we left the U.K. in 1965, and they were wonderful. We also had library books sent to us from the P.N.E.U., and we enjoyed those together too. They were great family times as, of course, the children were with us for a good bit of the day. We had a great giggle once when someone asked Penny, "What does your daddy do?" "Nothing," she replied!

I found an amusing quote from a letter of this time when Simon would have been 2½. (December 1966) I quote:

'Malcolm has just celebrated his 7th birthday with a lively party attended by Sunday School friends. His best friend is a scruffy little lad, son of a tinsmith brother of similar appearance. We found Hector in our bed, once, boots and all, but I may have mentioned that before. Friendships for missionary children are a real problem. Simon is keen to join in the school correspondence lessons. He also wants to take part in the Sunday School Anniversary on New Year's Day as Malcolm and Penny are doing so for the first time. His presence at that event promises to be as big a problem as it is at the rehearsals! He speaks a comical mixture of English and Spanish.'

When we finally left Bolivia at the end of 1969, we had some months in New Zealand, where all went to school. Malcolm sometimes says that was the only time when he was a normal schoolboy, living at home and going to school on weekdays. Although he looks on it as a happy time, he did have problems. The great disadvantage was that he didn't play football! He had never learned, and the other boys left him on the sideline.

In August we set out on the five week sea journey to England, arriving just in time to see Penny settled into Clarendon School and Malcolm into Scarisbrick Hall, both Christian boarding schools. The Lord had led us to continue our service for Him in Spain, and from there boarding school became a much more acceptable proposition. We were so wonderfully blessed. Because we were both working overseas, our Local Authority not only paid their fees but provided for them to come home to Spain for the holidays as well. Malcolm was ten years old and Penny nine. We found it heartrending to leave them at the great front doors of these two ancient mansions, but they both took to boarding school life incredibly well. This was, perhaps, partly because we had brought them up on the delightful skit on boarding school life called 'Down with School,' by Geoffrey Willans, and the adventures of Nigel Molesworth and his friends had kept our whole family giggling. It couldn't be that bad! They were relieved to find that it wasn't! Another important point was that we stressed to them the fact that only for the Lord's sake would we send them away from home, and I think that they accepted that. They were not in the position of so many of their school contemporaries who were sent to boarding school from broken families or just to get them out of the way.

Simon was only six when we went to Spain and could have integrated easily into a Spanish school, but we felt it was only fair to treat all three children the same to avoid any sense of favouritism or privilege. Accordingly Simon did the same correspondence course until he was ten, then he went to Scarisbrick

Hall as well. After teaching the older two mathematics using Imperial values (£.s.d.; lb. oz.; yards, feet and inches) it was such a joy to go Metric with Simon! I can remember Simon's protest sometimes in Spain if I took a bit of flexi-time and took him out with me. He had a very real sense of embarrassment at being in the street at a time when all Spanish children were in school. After two years, Scarisbrick Hall, having been a boys' school, opened its doors to girls and Penny transferred there. It was easier having all three in the same school as they had each other's support and the holidays were the same for all.

Unexpected problems arose which affected our missionary work. We were asked to help with summer camps which, of course, coincided with our own children being at home. For three years we spent several summer weeks in Galicia (in the NW of Spain) and our children joined us. Kind friends lent us their flat so that we could have something of the family life which our children missed during term time. One of us would take them to the beach in the morning, (while the other was leading the camp) and we would then join with camp activities in the afternoon and evening. This worked well for us but we discovered that it was not understood by everyone and we were criticised for 'not wanting our children to mix with theirs.' Nothing could be further from the truth but we decided to 'do our own thing' from then on. We bought a large family tent and spent some weeks each summer doing literature work on the beaches and in the markets of the Cantabrian coast of Spain. In that way the children had a family seaside holiday and we were able at the same time to continue with missionary work. From these weeks grew a very successful Bible correspondence work for children.

But I digress! This book is about Bolivia. Perhaps Spain will be a sequel one day. A long time later, but while we were still in Spain, Penny wrote the following poem which she and her husband Peter gave us for Christmas. They had written it on 'parchment' (which they nearly burnt in the oven!) and framed it. We treasure it to this day.

To Mum and Dad

"There is no one who has left house or parents or brothers or wife or children, for the sake of the kingdom of God, who shall not receive many times more…" Luke 18:29-30

~~~~~~~~~~~~~~~

You each those many years ago,
Left family and home
To serve the Lord in far off lands,
In distant places roam.
God kept His promise to restore
All things a hundredfold:
Each time our family reunites
There's happy memories told.
Again the sacrifice is made
As absent grandkids grow.
Still God is faithful to His Word:
Fresh blessings you will know.

—All our love, Peter, Penny and Matthew.
~~~~~~~~~~~~~~~

Culture Mix

Gordon and I were brought up in a typical British culture pattern, he in New Zealand and I in England. We learned courtesy, punctuality, fair play and respect for one's elders. We kept a stiff upper lip and kept back our tears. In the warmer clime of the Latin temperament, we came over as hard, cold and unfeeling. Our outward joy was not exuberant as was our neighbour's and, at funerals, we just couldn't cry floods of tears. Greetings were profuse in the Latin culture; between men and women it meant a bear-like hug followed by a hearty handshake and then another hug. Standing at the door of the hall to say 'goodbye' to each of the congregation was an endurance test, leaving one feeling sticky from grubby hands and totally dishevelled. I remember one rather fastidious missionary couple who made sure to wash their hands after just touching paper money. (This because of very doubtful toilet facilities; squatting in the gutter was the norm with no toilet paper or taps.)

Later when we were in Spain, the picture was very different. The Spanish people are very hygiene-conscious, putting us Brits to shame. There the usual greeting was a friendly kiss on both cheeks or, more formally, a kiss into the air on both sides somewhere in the region of the ear! A handshake was kept for very formal greetings. I was kissed by all manner of people in Spain, including even the boss of the removals firm who dealt with our furniture!

The Bolivian Indians have a very fine culture of their own, and some of the old men carried themselves in a really dignified manner. even though they were clothed in tattered garments. Something of the old Inca culture remains with them. If you go to visit, you don't knock on the door; rather you stand at a discreet distance and clap your hands loudly calling out, "Wasiyoj, wasiyoj!" ("Householder, householder!") In any case it was wise to stand first at a distance as they kept their dogs hungry! The Quechua children, while they were little rascals and many of them thieves, were lovely kids and we really enjoyed them. They would laugh with us rather than at us, but the town children were not so easy.

I remember, too, being very impressed when we first took a crowd of young people from Potosí to a few days conference in our home in Alcatuyo. On the first evening we met together to introduce ourselves all round. I was amazed at how each one stood up and, giving their name, said, "My name is_______, to serve all of you." I suppose we might say, "________at your service," but not quite with the warmth that they said it.

The national characteristics affect the YP too. It seems absolutely impossible for them to be on time, and many stroll in 45 minutes late. This means that a good bit of the planned programme cannot be carried out; then they wonder why the programme is not more varied! We have talked about it time and time again, and they all agree that it is a disgrace to be late, but it makes no difference. There is a saying here: 'hora boliviana,' and they live by it. It really means that any old time will do.

How easy it is to offend! It was only when we were about to leave Potosí for good that I discovered a point in which I must have been offending for many years. I gathered that it was considered most unladylike for a woman to cross her legs! Why didn't someone tell me before? I was very upset to think how often I must have caused offence in this way.

Gordon got into big trouble once, too, as he admired a lovely little boy saying,, "He's a real son of his father, isn't he?" It was meant to be complimentary, like saying, "Isn't he like his Dad?" but, oh dear! They took it as implying that he might *not* have been the son of his father!" I think it was the same man who surprised me and then was surprised in return. I was pregnant with Malcolm and suffering a lot of heartburn, when this good gentleman told me very seriously that it was because the baby's hair was twisted round my stomach. A novel idea! Imagine his surprise when, a week or two later, Malcolm was born as bald as a billiard ball! Bolivian babies arrive in this world with a thick mop of black hair.

Some Personal Stories

One always hopes and prays that there will be a response to the Gospel message and we shall see people young or old turn to the Lord for salvation. I was particularly anxious for those who helped me in the home. I wrote about Fortunata in Alcatuyo who was devoted to us as a family, but she never openly declared that she was saved. She may have been; I pray so. Perhaps the Lord will have brought another of His servants across her path who will have more success than I did. We had a succession of girls… Valeriana and Dominga (inherited from Mrs. Hamilton), Lily was with us for many years, Lucia often cared for the children when they were small, Marina, and then Leonor and Atiana together. Some were believers, some not. Here are some stories about a few of them.

~~~~~~~~~~~~~~~~~~

I can't remember the name of the girl who came to me one evening after supper. She wanted a word with me alone. 'Perhaps this is it!' I thought, but I was quickly disillusioned when she told me how desperately anxious she was to travel overseas. She then unfolded a plan; she would accompany us when we go on furlough, helping where necessary but living with us for evermore and looking on us as father and mother! I spent the whole evening trying to explain tactfully that the idea was absurd, but she wouldn't be persuaded. Gordon will have the unhappy task of saying, "No, definitely no," and I fear we may not see her at YPF again, though I may be misjudging her. I hope so.

~~~~~~~~~~~~~~~~~~

TERESA

We took in a lodger! We didn't mean to. It all happened because we got to know a school teacher in Yocalla last year and she seemed interested in the Gospel. During the holidays she came to my ladies' meeting on Tuesdays, and a month ago she was saved. Then she had to return to Yocalla with the younger children. The husband is away studying in La Paz and this lady was at her wit's end to find a home for her 14 year old daughter who has to stay in town for secondary school. No one would take the responsibility for a girlie of her age. We, like a couple of warm hearted mugs, offered to do so! She has been with us for three weeks. The first two weeks were dreadful, and we decided we would really have to hand Teresa back to her mother. She escaped from the house for long periods (she can't tell the time properly) and was never punctual for meals. Twice Gordon had to go out looking for her. She was a Catholic girl and resisted heartily all our efforts to get her to meetings. She did come eventually but we feared it would be a battle each week.

During week three, her behaviour improved considerably and we became quite fond of her as she is a sweet, bright girl. Yesterday, to my amazement, she brought a friend to the meeting and made no fuss. Then, while she was helping me to wash up the cups after YPF she suddenly said to me, "Señora, how do you accept the Lord?" We sat down to talk about it and she did accept the Lord as her Saviour. We had prayed so much for her, but I must confess that we were quite taken aback by such a sudden change of heart.

Next morning, as she went off to school, she told Leonor and Atiana that she had a 'second birthday,' 7th April.

~~~~~~~~~~~~~~~~~~~~

LEONOR and ATIANA

These two girls came to work for us at the same time. Leonor was 13 and Atiana I think only 12. They were thrilled to bits to come and work for us and to earn some money to help in their very poor homes. They went to evening classes in dressmaking afterwards. They hadn't a clue, of course! Atiana must have cost us more in breakages than to pay her salary, and Leonor seemed
~~~~~~~~~~~~~~~~~~~~

to cut herself every time she picked up a knife, so was always bandaged or plastered. As Teresa left the house having dropped this bombshell about her birthday, Leonor and Atiana said, "She's a fibber isn't she? Her birthday is in October." I took the opportunity to explain to them how a person can be 'born again,' and thus have a second birthday, and that this is what had happened to Teresa. I quote from a letter: 'They asked me about it this afternoon and just now, Leonor, who comes from a Christian home, has accepted the Lord too. Atiana, also from a Christian home, decided to wait for two months, but if the Lord comes she will make the decision and get saved quickly! I pointed out the danger of such a decision, but don't want to push her into being saved just to be like the other two girls. Another of my S.S. class, Filomena, was caught stealing and has been sent to a convent to cure her!'

~~~~~~~~~~~~~~~~~~~~~~

JUDITH and more of ATIANA

Judith was a granddaughter of believers. I quote a letter: "Judith was a girl of 21 who sometimes accompanied her mother to meetings, though she seemed to have a rather rebellious spirit. She has had every opportunity to hear the Gospel from babyhood but, although she did once make a profession, there has never been any sign of spiritual life, and we doubt whether she was genuine. One day, Judith contracted meningitis, and about a week later she died. She certainly hadn't expected to die so soon and her death made a tremendous impression on her contemporaries. The funeral was very big and sad indeed. Judith had been chosen as 'Queen' of the most prestigious boy's college and the boys turned out with the school banner, as did the girls of her own college. The coffin had a glass top and I saw that she had been dressed in her crown, a tinselly thing, and one could not help but contrast it with the crowns the Lord offers to those who faithfully serve Him.

I commented on Judith's funeral to Leonor and Atiana. Teresa no longer lives with us. I think it was Judith's sudden death that
~~~~~~~~~~~~~~~~~~~~~~

clinched it for Atiana and now, to our joy, she has come to the Lord for salvation as well. She made the decision alone, though I think our young Malcolm may have been talking to her. Our children have been very anxious for her, and when she eventually told us, she had come to the Lord, Penny sighed with relief and said, 'Now it doesn't matter if we get gassed, we'll **all** go to Heaven!' (She has always been worried about our Calor gas cooker!)

Pennies from Heaven?

Questions were often put to us by well-meaning friends and well-wishers. "How were you financed?" "Where did the funds come from?" "Who paid your salary?" Our answer that the Lord provides for our needs (not necessarily our 'wants') and we just trust Him, was beyond the understanding of many. It was harder still to explain to the authorities! I don't think they were too concerned in Bolivia, foreign money was always welcome, but in Spain the local authorities and the taxman all wanted us to explain ourselves. We would always be asked:

Who is your employer?	Answer:	God!
What is your monthly salary?	Answer:	No idea!

Going back to the beginning, in my case, I had left Nursing and received superannuation, a very modest sum. This was quickly used up in preparations for the journey. The boat fare was a lot of money but I managed to pay that. Just at that time I chanced upon a very serious little poem:

> 'Hast thou wherewith to pay thy fare? Well be it so.
> It may cost what thou knowest not
> To bring thee home from there.'
> —(Author unknown)

I had no idea about taking money overseas so I decided to visit the Bank Manager. I was scared but it seemed as though the Lord had taken me by the hand. The Manager listened to my story and then asked, "Why do you want to go to Bolivia?" As soon as I told him, he stood and shook my hand. "I'm a Christian too," he said, "so I know exactly what you mean." This was in 1957 when sending money overseas was very carefully controlled. The Manager explained that all I was allowed to take in cash was $US100.00 I cannot remember the exchange rate at the time, but I had nothing like that much money! "Well," said the Manager, "we'll order $US 100.00 for you and trust the Lord to send that much into your account by the time it comes." There were only three weeks to go, but I had that money in time. Doesn't the Lord have His servants in the right places?

Another wonderful thing that happened while I was preparing (though not in matters of finance) was connected with my visa. I had got my passport while I was doing the Assimilation Course of the Wycliffe Summer Institute of Linguistics, but there remained the business of getting a visa for Bolivia. I went fearfully to the Bolivian Embassy in London and was ushered into an office. The two Bolivian officials who were there, on hearing my name said, "Oh we've been waiting for you!" I couldn't believe my ears. I found that Dr. Brown (with whom I had been corresponding) had applied for and been granted all the necessary permits on my behalf. I had no idea of all that was going on. So my passport was immediately stamped with the appropriate permits and there was nothing to hinder my progress. I could not doubt that the Lord was leading me. I had to go! The Lord had abundantly answered my question, the title of this book: "Must I really go, Lord?"

Once in Bolivia no one could send gifts of money directly to me. This is where 'Echoes of Service' came in (and they are still on the job with the present generation). I want to make it clear that we were not paid by Echoes! They are a body of Christian gentlemen who are called by the Lord to their responsibilities, even as we were called to the Mission Field. In those days, when it was difficult to get money overseas, they were a recognised channel by which this could be done. They passed on to me (and later to us) all monetary gifts which were sent to them, earmarked for me, in full, without any deductions, not even for office expenses. They also distribute other monies, such as legacies, according to their knowledge of the needs of the workers and the cost of living in the countries in which they are working. Now, in the year 2000+, they do many more things, such as visiting the missionaries on the field to 'see how they do.' They produce their own books to tell of their activities. Echoes also take very seriously the responsibility of praying for all the missionaries with whom they have contact and of making a list of these people available to churches, assemblies and individuals. This means that they need to be sure that all the missionaries with whom they have to do are truly saved and baptised, that they are called of the Lord Himself, and will faithfully teach the Word of God. They do not presume to direct the missionaries in any way. Gordon and I really appreciated this as we compared our lot with those of some missions whose workers were salaried and told where to go and what to do. We were free to do as the Lord led us, and while we were, of course, accountable first to the Lord and then to our assemblies at home, we were not expected to send in statistics. Although we were not salaried and lived by faith, we found we were better supported than many of our missionary friends from other groups.

We were each commended to the Lord's service as missionaries to Bolivia, by our home assemblies, the Christians who knew us best. We had worshipped and lived and worked amongst them, Gordon at Eden Chapel in Auckland, NZ, and I at Montpelier Hall in Purley, Surrey. I had been at Montpelier from 8 years old so, they knew me pretty well! I had been amongst those who started up a Young People's meeting after the war years and, under the Lord's hand, it grew and prospered. I was an officer in many Crusader and assembly camps. When I did ask the elders of the assembly if they would be willing to commend me to Bolivia, they were wonderfully kind and encouraging to me. It was they who passed my name to Echoes of Service, and who supported me financially and prayerfully, very faithfully over the whole of my missionary life (1957 – 1997). I cannot thank them enough.

We soon proved that what the Lord sent would cover all our needs, even large ones such as a car! We had many extraordinary experiences of the Lord's provision. In one of the chapters of this book I described how the Land Rover became ours. We hadn't the money but, when we went to the Post Office in Potosí, there were some unexpected items, including a legacy from a lady unknown to us, and, counting all we had, we were able to go and purchase the Land Rover (second hand) straight away. The Lord had kept it for us for several weeks.

The Lord always knew when we needed a car! It happened in Spain as well. When we first went there in 1971, we looked around for a second hand car. Friends showed us a 'bargain' but, as we came away after a test drive, Gordon said, "I'm sure the Lord has something better for us than that!" A day or two later a very big cheque arrived from a long-standing friend of mine, with a note to say, "I'm sure you'll be in need of a car. Here is some help towards it." With what we already had set by, we were able to pay for a brand new car, though without tax, as tourists. When the time came to pay the tax, the same lady sent that money too. Years later, quite recently in fact, she told me that she had been standing at a bus stop when the Lord said to her, "The Bissets need a car!" Can anything be more personal than that?

Some years later, when the children had grown, their school luggage or our camping equipment proved too much for the car, and something vital (I am no mechanic!) broke underneath! The Lord saw to it that this should happen near to a small town where there was a suitable mechanic to deal with it, but we realised that the time had come to pray for a new car! We only told the Lord. Again He spoke to the same lady (poor thing!) and again a cheque came from her with a note, "You must be in need of a larger car now that the children are bigger!" By the next time we needed another new car, we had inherited some money from our parents, so we felt it wasn't right to bother the Lord about it as we had the money already in the Bank!

In Spain, too, on another occasion, we had to pay the insurance on the car, the sum of 26,000 pesetas. We hadn't got that much money in the Bank. We knew that there was a cheque on the way through Echoes, but it didn't arrive. What could we do? Pray of course! Gordon went to the Bank once again. No, nothing had come in to our account. The clerk said, "Come back tomorrow and I will see if I can trace the cheque for you by then." Next day, Gordon went into the Bank again and (oh joy!) the money had come. But that was not all. Overnight the peseta had been devalued and we got 26,000 pesetas more for it than we would have done the previous day! Just the right amount for the car insurance.

Another occasion comes to mind, in Bolivia. We were short of money, and this time no miracles happened. The only thing to do was to sell some bits and pieces. We had doubled up on several items when we got married, so those were the first to go. We had to sell some of our furniture as well, and we were not so happy about this. However, it wasn't too long before we moved house yet again and 'Hey Presto!' our furniture fitted exactly on to the truck we had hired! Not a stick of what we had sold would have gone on it.

Living by faith is the surest way there is of having enough, and sometimes abundance! We can heartily recommend it.

~~~~~~~~~~~~~~~~~

I have mentioned only 'Echoes of Service' as they were the missionary service agency who cared for me. Gordon, having been commended from New Zealand, was cared for through 'Missionary Funds, New Zealand' (now called 'Global Connections in Mission'). There are similar entities in other countries:
~~~~~~~~~~~~~~~~~

'Christian Missions in Many Lands' in USA,
'MSC CANADA' in Canada, and,
'Australian Missionary Tidings' in Australia.

All these collaborate fully in the Lord's work overseas.